D1594138

The
Jackson Hole
Bachelor's Cookbook

By Sparky J. Imeson

Aurora Publications

7440 White Ash Place
Parker, Colorado 80134-5464

The
Jackson Hole
Bachelor's Cookbook

By Sparky J. Imeson

Published by:

Aurora Publications
7440 White Ash Place
Parker, Colorado 80134-5464

Copyright © 1991, by Sparky J. Imeson
First Edition
First printing: September 1991
Printed in the United States of America

ISBN 1-880568-11-X $8.95 Softcover

Table of Contents

About The Author

Sparky J. Imeson was born and raised in Jackson, Wyoming. He grew up in the mountains where his grandfather homesteaded, enjoying hunting, fishing and camping. Camping—as a Boy Scout—was his introduction to cooking. Sparky and Philip "Butch" Garetson were the first boys to attend a home economics class (that's where all the girls were) at the Jackson-Wilson High School.

Sparky is not a chef and does not profess to be one. He just enjoys cooking and likes to share his knowledge and experience with others that express enthusiasm in the kitchen. His vocation is that of a pilot, logging over 14,600 hours in small airplanes during the past 23 years. His avocation is writing.

In 1969, as part owner of an FBO (fixed base operator—airplane sales and rentals, fuel, maintenance, training, charter, ambulance, spraying and aerobatic training) in Jackson, he became alarmed at the number of aircraft accidents attributed to mountain flying. He couldn't find a book on the subject so he sat down and wrote *Mountain Flying*.

Other books by Sparky include *Private Pilot Flight Training Guide*, 1972; *Instrument Training Guide*, 1973; *Private-Commercial Learning Guide*, 1974; *Instrument Flying Handbook*, 1974; *Professional Pilot Training*, 1974; *Introduction to Aerobatic Flight*, 1976; *Private Pilot (Airplane) Flight Training Guide*, 1988; *Instrument Pilot (Airplane) Flight Training Guide*, 1988; *SkyGuide® Flight Operations Handbook*, 1991; *The Mountain Flying Bible*, 1991.

Sparky was encouraged to write this book by his many firends who wanted to obtain recipes developed by Ron Schultz. Sparky Never kept "secret" recipes and was glad to share, but found it to be a hassle to write down all of Ron's recipes over and over. He has revealed many of Ron's unwritten secrets—enjoy!

Preface

To prevent any misconceptions, it is best to set matters straight before we begin. I am not a professional chef or baker. I simply love good food and I love to cook. I earn my living as a pilot and author of aviation books.

My first love, after my wife and daughters, is flying; and, sometimes Darlene claims I love those darn airplanes more than I do her. My next love is cooking. The title of this book might be misleading, as I was married before I got my calling to the kitchen. My bride knew how to make tuna-fish sandwiches. But, even one in love can't face tuna-fish sandwiches day after day, so I whipped up an omelette—it was unbelievably easy and surprisingly good. During the years, with practice and experimentation I have improved on it, but not much.

Before we go farther let me state that my wife is now an excellent cook. I don't want to cook every meal and I don't have to. This is the advantage a bachelor has over a housewife; he can choose when and what he wants to cook—there isn't the daily drag of having to prepare well-balanced meals for a family. After you've discovered your talents with herbs, spices and wines, you won't want to settle for a TV dinner ever again.

During my college years, I worked in a pizza house and had a following who would come in just to watch me twirl, stretch and toss the pizza dough. These days I don't waste my time making pizza, as one can purchase a ready-made in almost any city. While it is a fun thing to do, it is very time consuming for the results.

In those college years, while working as a policeman, I also learned to make Mexican foods from my partner and best friend, Vince Valdez—who got his know-how direct from Mexico. His green chili was so hot a glass of water would taste like cayenne pepper three days later. I have included some of those recipes, cooled down for American palates.

Another dear friend, Ron Schultz, taught me many of my secrets. Ron was my next door neighbor and one of the owners of the Million Dollar Cowboy Bar in Jackson, Wyoming. Ron and I visited on a daily basis and he soon took pity on my attempt at cooking. He took me "under his wing" and taught me how to make something palatable. He has passed away, but lives on in my kitchen.

Ron worked for Harrah's Club, Reno, and travelled all over Europe getting food ideas for their kitchens. Ron wasn't a true chef

in the sense that he received a diploma from some prestigious cooking school, but he was a chef in his food preparations and creations.

Ron never used a cookbook or written recipe, but by watching him and tasting (and writing everything down), I learned how an infinitesimal pinch of a special herb changes a ho-hum dish to a production. And, Ron knew how to use wines. He said, "Don't use a cheap wine to cook with. Don't be afraid to experiment . . . and a little nip of the wine now and then, for the cook, always improves the dish."

My mom inspired my cooking to a great extent by allowing me free access to the kitchen. Besides being an excellent cook, she has a knack for experimenting and coming up with some mouth-teasing creations.

Most bachelors would like to think of themselves as *gourmets*, but shrink away from cooking as they do not realize how easy it is to prepare taste-tickling treats. Whereas the true "gourmet" is a connoisseur (informed and astute judge in matters of taste) of fine food and drink, we less informed can fully appreciate fine foods as much as the connoisseur. Even many experienced housewives have hangups thinking about making a pie crust or a soufflé. Read on, and I will show you how easy it is.

Don't try for a seven or twelve course dinner, especially when first embarking on your culinary career. In flying we use the letters of words to remember important data (acronyms). KISS (keep it simple, stupid) is just as important in the kitchen as in the air. Better to have just one specialty lovingly tended and served with a salad, than to have many mediocre choices. If it is a hot dish, serve it piping hot; or a cold dish, have it well chilled.

Also, I have learned to bake bread, rolls and muffins from scratch, but unless you have an undercover reason for doing it, don't. It is time consuming and mixes are easy and reliable. Most bakeries put out good ready-made, and if you drop them in a paper bag and pop them in the oven for a few minutes, they serve well. French bread can be sliced in fairly thick diagonal slices, spread with garlic butter and grilled until faintly brown and toasted. Or, if you would rather not have it crispy, when slicing, don't pass through the crust at the bottom. This will hold the loaf together and after smearing with garlic butter, wrap in aluminum foil and leave in a 350° oven for about 10 minutes.

Pie is a different matter. You must make your own if you want a superior product. The crust is what takes the time and trouble, so I usually make several at once and freeze the surplus, with or without the filling.

Most of the recipes in this book are for four to eight people, assuming you want to share your triumphs. This book is not a cooking encyclopedia; its purpose is to present some of my finest recipes and prove you do not have to be a chef to prepare gourmet cooking. Experiments belong in the kitchen. If at the last minute the meal is not the success you hoped for, that is the only time to push the bar before dinner. Usually you will keep drinks and nibbles light so your production will be fully appreciated.

You may encounter terms in this and other recipe books which are unfamiliar to you. If *cut in, mince,* or *coddle* doesn't have any meaning for you, check the *Procedures and Definitions* section beginning on page 73.

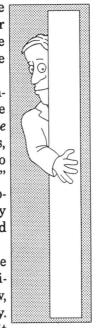

During review of the manuscript, a few people commented some of the recipes given do not appear to be indigenous to Jackson Hole. So, why the name, *The Jackson Hole Bachelor's Cookbook*? All I can say is, "Gee, I was born and raised in Jackson Hole, learned to cook in Jackson, and these are the recipes we cooked."

Yes, indeed, the bachelor in Jackson Hole has progressed in the last few years. Time was when he only knew how to cook a kettle of beans, fry an elk steak and burn some sour-dough biscuits.

I'm not going to tell you how to cook a fish in the dishwasher or any other far-out complexities. My recipes are honest, tried and repeated good eating. Now, let's grab an apron and get down to the nitty-gritty. (Yeah, guys, it's okay to wear an apron . . . as long as it isn't too frilly.)

ACKNOWLEDGMENT

I sincerely thank my wife, Darlene, and my mother, Jennie, for their contributions and suggestions. I also thank Babette André and Sonia Best for their information and copy editing.

Appetizers

ANTIPASTO PLATTER

tomato slices	melon caps
watermelon caps	radishes
sunflower nuts	green pepper slices
carrots	celery sticks
green onions	mushroom pieces or slices
hot peppers	black olives

☐ Slice your choice of the above and arrange on a dish. Serve with blue cheese dressing or your favorite dip.

CLAM DIP

2 3-oz pkgs cream cheese   ½ tsp. onion - grated
1 6-8-oz can minced clams   salt
½ tsp. Worcestershire sauce

☐ Beat cream cheese, adding onion and Worcestershire sauce.

☐ Drain and reserve clam juice. Add clams to mixture.

☐ Add clam juice for dip consistency.

☐ Salt to taste.

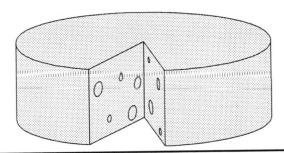

ROTEL CHEESE DIP

2 pound block *Velveeta* cheese
1 can *Rotel* Tomatoes with green chilies
1 bag tortilla chips (or corn chips)

☐ Place the *Velveeta* cheese in a double boiler. Cut into chunks to facilitate melting.

☐ Pour can of *Rotel* tomatoes and green chilies over the cheese.

☐ Place double boiler on medium heat until the cheese melts.

☐ Serve with chips.

☞ This is the easiest of appetizers to make, yet it is surprisingly good. The cheese will thicken as it cools making it desirable to place it in a fondue pot or chafing dish on low heat.

☞ The dip can be made without a double boiler, but must be constantly stirred to keep from burning the cheese. If the dip is not consumed, it can be refrigerated and reheated later.

UNCLE RON'S ESCARGOT AND MUSHROOMS

6½ ounce can Escargot
½ pound fresh mushrooms
    butter
    oil
½ medium onion — diced
½ bay leaf

1 teaspoon parsley flakes
½ teaspoon oregano
¾ tsp. Worcestershire sauce
2 garlic cloves, chopped
½ teaspoon Italian seasoning

☐ Dice onions, slice mushrooms and escargot. *Slice the escargot diagonally into 1/8-inch thick pieces to disguise the snails if you encounter a guest that doesn't think they like them. You'll be surprised how much they do like them.*

☐ Add enough butter to a frying pan on high heat to make a liquid 3/16-inch deep. Add 2 tablespoons oil to keep the butter from burning.

☐ Add diced onions, parsley flakes, oregano, Worcestershire sauce, garlic and Italian seasoning. Cook until the onions are soft (they turn colorless or nearly so).

☐ Add sliced mushrooms and escargot. Simmer 8 minutes.

☐ Serve in dish with toothpicks or cocktail forks.

GUACAMOLE DIP

4	ripe avocados	¾	cup sour cream
½	teaspoon diced jalapeños	1	small onion, diced
2	tomatoes, chopped fine	1	teaspoon lemon juice
1	teaspoon sugar	¼	teaspoon chili powder
¼	teaspoon Durkee RedHot		paprika
	salt		coarse ground pepper

☐ Peel and mash avocados (if using a blender for mixing, slice avocados into chunks).

☐ Add all ingredients except paprika and mix well.

☐ Salt and pepper to taste.

☐ Sprinkle small amount of paprika over top.

☞ To peel and seed avocados, slice into the center until encountering the seed. Turn the avocado until sliced all around. Pull the two halves apart. Remove and retain one seed. Slide a tablespoon between the skin and meat and move all around the edges, then scoop the meat out.

☞ If the dip is to be refrigerated for any amount of time, place one avocado seed in the center, immersed half way, to keep the dip from turning dark colored.

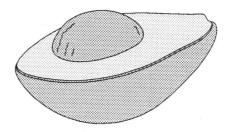

> Insert a steel or aluminum nail (clean, of course) into a potato from end to end to reduce the baking time by 15 minutes.

CRAB STUFFED MUSHROOMS

1½ lbs large fresh mushrooms 1 cube butter
½ cup bread crumbs ½ cup green onions—sliced thin
8 oz. canned crab meat ½ cup fresh parsley—chopped
¾ cup Parmesan cheese ½ lb. Velveeta cheese—grated
salt (very little) pepper (to taste)

☐ Wash the mushrooms in cold water and remove the stems to form a cavity in the mushroom cap.

☐ Place mushroom caps (top side up) on paper towels to drain.

☐ To prepare the stuffing: melt the butter, add the bread crumbs, green onions, crab meat, parsley, Parmesan, *Velveeta*, and a small portion of salt and pepper. Stir to obtain a consistent mixture (it will be thick).

☐ Lightly oil a casserole dish.

☐ Using a spoon and your fingers, stuff the mushroom caps and place them in the oiled casserole dish.

☐ Sprinkle an additional amount of Parmesan cheese (¼ cup at most) on top.

☐ Bake in an oven at 325° for 45 minutes.

☞ Lightly oil a casserole dish: Put your hand in a plastic bag or baggie and spread a thin coating of Crisco vegetable shortening on the bottom and sides.

BABY BACK PORK RIBS

¼ to ½ pounds pork ribs per guest

☞ Try *Mountain Man Barbecue Sauce* (page 36)

☐ Barbecue the ribs on low heat until well done, basting frequently with the sauce.

☐ After cooking, slice the ribs into small portions and baste again.

☐ Serve immediately.

☞ When basting the ribs the coals will probably flare up. Pour a little water on the fire whenever needed and continue cooking. This applies to gas grills also.

RUMAKI (BACON WRAPPED WATER CHESTNUTS)

water chestnuts	soy sauce
bacon	white sugar

☐ Wrap bacon slices around water chestnuts and use toothpicks to hold.

☐ Dip prepared water chestnuts in soy sauce and roll in sugar.

☐ Bake until bacon is done.

SHRIMP DIP (OR CRAB)

8 oz package cream cheese	1 can tomato soup
½ cup diced onion	¾ cup mayonnaise
2 teaspoons lemon juice	½ cup chopped celery
1 tsp. Worcestershire sauce	¼ teaspoon garlic powder
2 6½ oz cans shrimp (or crab)	

☐ Melt cream cheese and tomato soup together.

☐ Mix ingredients well.

☐ Refrigerate to chill before serving.

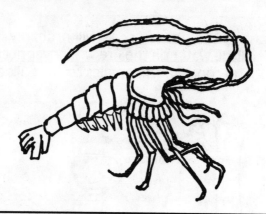

UNCLE RON'S SHRIMP SCAMPI

1 pound shrimp (fresh or frozen) — large size
Imitation butter flavored salt

butter	soy sauce
garlic juice	garlic salt
Beau Monde	Mr. Pepper
parsley flakes	fresh lemon

❒ Spread the shrimp on a double thickness of paper towels. Sprinkle a small portion of soy sauce (not too much, it's salty) over the shrimp. Immediately turn the shrimp so the soy sauce is absorbed into the towels.

❒ Place a frying pan over high heat. Add enough butter to make a 1/16 -inch thickness. Add 2 tablespoons oil to keep the butter from burning.

❒ Place shrimp in pan. Sprinkle about 10 drops of garlic juice and a very light sprinkling of garlic salt into the pan. Sprinkle beau monde, Mr. Pepper and parsley flakes on the shrimp. Add small amount of imitation butter flavored salt. Squeeze fresh lemon over shrimp (use a cloth around the lemon to keep the seeds from falling into the pan).

❒ When the sauce boils, reduce heat and simmer 3 to 4 minutes, turning shrimp occasionally.

☞ Serve with garlic butter and parsley or cocktail sauce. Don't overcook the shrimp. Using a large bowl, place a cup of sauce in the center and hang the shrimp over the edge of the bowl.

UNCLE RON'S SHRIMP AND MUSHROOMS

½ pound medium size shrimp (fresh or frozen)
⅓ pound fresh mushrooms   butter
½ med size onion — diced   oil
1 teaspoon parsley flakes   ½ teaspoon oregano
¾ tsp. Worcestershire sauce ½ teaspoon Italian seasoning
2 garlic cloves — squeezed or chopped

❑ Dice onions and slice mushrooms.

❑ Add butter to frying pan on high heat until (liquid) ³/₁₆ - inch deep. Add 2 tablespoons oil (keep the butter from burning).

❑ Add diced onions, parsley flakes, oregano, Worcestershire sauce, garlic and Italian seasoning. Cook until onions are soft.

❑ Add sliced mushrooms and shrimp. Simmer 3 to 4 minutes.

❑ Serve in a dish with toothpicks or cocktail forks.

UNCLE RON'S SHRIMP CURRIE

¾ pound medium size shrimp (fresh or frozen)
1 tablespoon soy sauce   ½ medium onion — diced
1 tbsp. teriyaki sauce   1 tbsp. *Madras* curry powder
½ cup milk   ½ tsp. parsley flakes
¼ tsp. all purpose Greek seasoning
¼ teaspoon *Mr. Pepper*   ½ tsp. *Old Bay* Seasoning
½ teaspoon corn starch

❑ Dice onions.

❑ Add shrimp, soy sauce and onions to frying pan.

❑ Blend Teriyaki sauce, curry powder and milk in a bowl. Add to frying pan and place on high heat.

❑ Mix parsley, Greek seasoning, Mr. Pepper, Old Bay and corn starch in small bowl. Sprinkle over shrimp when mixture begins to boil.

❑ Immediately reduce heat and simmer 4 minutes.

Beverages

UNCLE RON'S BLOODY MARY

1 dash *Kikkoman Japanese Style Steak Sauce*
1 dash *Tabasco*
½ teaspoon lime juice
   salt to taste
   pepper to taste
   tomato juice
   vodka, as desired
   top with celery salt

❑ Mix ingredients in a glass, stir and serve with a celery stalk.

UNCLE RON'S IRISH CREAM

To make an Irish cream which rivals *Bailey's Original Irish Cream* in consistency and taste:

1 can *Eagle* brand milk
1 heaping teaspoon cocoa
3 ounce *Kahlúa*
¼ bottle of whiskey (fifth)

❑ Mix ingredients together, then add:

1 pint half and half

❑ Keep refrigerated.

MARGARITA

1 12-oz can frozen lime juice
8 oz tequila (½ juice can)   1 fresh lime
4 oz Triple Sec (¼ juice can)   margarita salt
1½ tsp. brown sugar   1 cup ice

❑ In a blender, place frozen lime juice, tequila, Triple Sec, brown sugar and ice.

❑ Cut lime into 4 wedges.

❑ Rub lime around rim of glass and dip rim of glass into margarita salt to coat, squeezing remainder of lime wedge into glass.

❑ Strain margarita mixture into glass.

Salads

ORIGINAL CAESAR SALAD

10 Romaine lettuce leaves
6 ½-inch slices french bread
2½ tablespoons garlic oil
3 garlic cloves
6 anchovy fillets
1 egg
1 tablespoon lime juice
1 teaspoon Worcestershire sauce
¼ cup parmesan cheese — grated
salt and pepper

☐ Preheat oven to 400°. Bake French bread 5 minutes on ungreased baking sheet. Brush with 1½ tablespoons garlic oil and bake 15 minutes.

☐ Place egg (in shell) in boiling water and coddle (cook just below the boiling point) for 1 minute.

☐ Rub the inside edges of a wooden bowl with garlic.

☐ In a small rounded bowl, place garlic cloves, anchovy and 1 tablespoon garlic oil. Crush together and spread on French bread.

☐ Cut bread into cubes and set aside.

☐ Place lettuce, lime juice, Worcestershire, cheese, egg and cubed bread in bowl and toss. Salt and pepper to taste.

☞ This is the original Caesar Salad as developed by Caesar Cardini, an Italian restaurateur, at the Caesar Hotel in Tijuana, Mexico. Caesar was joined in the hotel/restaurant business by his brother Alex who was a World War I ace pilot in the Italian Air Force. As an honor to the pilots at the San Diego air base, Alex modified his brother's salad with other ingredients and called it Aviator's Salad. But, this popular dish became internationally known as Caesar Salad.

CAESAR SALAD (TRADITIONAL)

10	Romaine lettuce leaves	1	tablespoon lime juice
2½	tablespoons garlic oil	1	tsp. Worcestershire sauce
3	garlic cloves	¼	cup parmesan cheese—grated
6	anchovy fillets	1	cup croutons
1	egg — coddled		salt and pepper

❏ Crush the garlic by laying a knife over them sideways and pushing down. Remove the skin and place in a large wooden bowl. Use two forks to mash and grind the garlic cloves together until shredded fine. Rub into the sides of the bowl.

❏ Use the two forks to mash and grind the anchovy fillets into small pieces.

❏ Add garlic oil, egg, lime juice, Worcestershire and 1/8 cup of parmesan cheese to bowl and mix.

❏ Add lettuce leaves and toss.

❏ Salt and pepper to taste.

❏ Sprinkle remaining 1/8 cup of parmesan cheese over top.

❏ Serve immediately.

COLESLAW
Sauce:

½	cup mayonnaise	⅓	cup sugar
8	ounces sour cream	3	tablespoons vinegar
1½	teaspoon salt	2	teaspoons dry mustard
2	teaspoons grated onion		

❏ Mix ingredients for sauce together.

1½	lbs cabbage, shredded	½	lbs red cabbage, shredded
2	carrots, shredded	½	cup raisins

❏ Mix cabbage, carrots and raisins. Place half in bowl and pour half of the sauce over it.

❏ Add remainder of cabbage mixture to bowl and pour remainder of sauce over it.

❏ Press down with large spoon.

❏ Cover and refrigerate several hours to blend flavors.

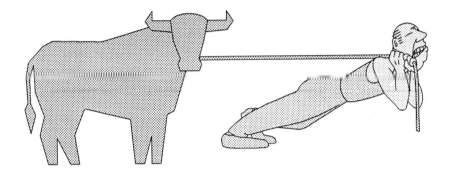

TACO SALAD

1	pound lean ground beef
1	head lettuce — shredded
1	large tomato — sliced into wedges
½	red onion — diced
½	yellow onion — diced
½	green pepper — diced
½	cup black olives — diced
½	pound sharp cheddar cheese — grated
1	cup Miracle Whip
½	cup *La Victoria* Salsa Supreme
8	ounces tortilla chips — crushed

❏ Cook the ground beef and drain off the fat. Crumble meat. Cool to room temperature.

❏ Toss the salad combining lettuce, tomato, onions, green pepper, olives and cheese. Add meat when cool.

❏ Mix dressing (Miracle Whip and Salsa Supreme) and add.

❏ Sprinkle tortilla chips over the top.

❏ Serve chilled.

Getting catsup out of a stubborn bottle—Remember Newton's Law that *every action has an equal and opposite reaction?* Instead of hitting down while holding the bottle inverted, try hitting up with the palm of your hand on the side of the bottle. It should start the flow. If it doesn't, insert a drinking straw to the bottom of the bottle to admit some air and start the flow.

Soups

UNCLE RON'S BEEF STEW

1½ lbs beef stew meat (leftover roast), cut into 1-inch cubes

¼ cup flour	¾ teaspoons salt
¼ teaspoon pepper	1½ tablespoons cooking oil

- ☐ Mix flour, salt and pepper in a plastic bag, add meat and shake.
- ☐ Brown beef cubes in hot oil using Dutch oven or other heavy pan.
- ☐ Pour off fat.

2½	cups water	¾	teaspoon salt
2	bay leaves	1	teaspoons oregano, ground
1	tsp. coriander, ground	1	teaspoon cumin, ground
¼	teaspoon pepper	1	clove garlic, minced
½	teaspoon thyme	1	teaspoon allspice
4	carrots, cut in chunks	3	potatoes, peeled and cubed
2	large onions, quartered	3	celery stalks, diced
2	tomatoes, peeled and quartered (or 16 oz. can stewed tomatoes)		

1	12-oz can V-8 juice (regular or spicy-hot)
½	cup white wine -or- 1 can beer (optional)
¼	cup water
4	tablespoons cornstarch (or all purpose flour)

- ☐ Add all ingredients (except ¼ cup water and 4 tablespoons cornstarch). Bring to boil; reduce heat and cover. Simmer about 1¼ hours.
- ☐ Remove bay leaves and skim off any fat.
- ☐ Place ¼ cup water and 4 tablespoons cornstarch in small jar and shake until well mixed. Stir slowly into meat mixture to thicken stew.
- ☐ Cover and simmer ½ hour.
- ☐ Serve with green salad and garlic bread.

☞ If a Dutch oven is not available, place all ingredients in a stock pot or crock pot to cook.

ONION SOUP

4	large onions, thinly sliced	1	tablespoon butter
1	tablespoon vegetable oil	¼	teaspoon sugar
2	tablespoons flour	6	cups bouillon
¼	cup dry white wine		salt and pepper
2	teaspoons vegetable oil	1	clove garlic, minced
2	tablespoons cognac	1	cup grated Swiss cheese
4	slices French bread, cut ½-inch thick		

☐ In covered saucepan or Dutch oven, cook onions slowly with butter and 1 tablespoon oil for 15 minutes. Stir occasionally.

☐ Uncover, increase heat to moderate and add sugar.

☐ Sauté onions, stirring frequently for about 30 minutes or until golden brown. Sprinkle with flour. Stir for 2 to 3 minutes. Blend in hot broth and wine. Add seasonings. Simmer, partially covered for 1 hour.

☐ Place bread slices in 350° oven for 30 minutes. Halfway through baking, baste each slice with ½ teaspoon oil and garlic mixture.

☐ Add cognac and divide soup into 4 ovenproof bowls. Sprinkle ½ cup cheese in soup. Float slices of toasted French bread on soup. Sprinkle with rest of cheese.

☐ Bake in preheated 325° oven 15 to 20 minutes. Set under broiler 2 to 3 minutes until cheese is golden brown.

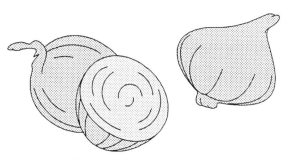

When cooking meat (especially steaks)—Do not add salt until just before removing from the stove, oven or grill; otherwise, it will tend to make the meat tough.

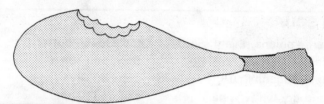

UNCLE RON'S TURKEY SOUP

1	turkey carcass with some meat		
2	onions — sliced	1	teaspoon salt
1	teaspoon pepper	1½	teaspoon parsley flakes
20	chicken bouillon cubes	½	teaspoon yellow food color
1	small potato—sliced thin	4	ounces extra wide noodles

❑ Place turkey carcass (it might be necessary to cut it into smaller pieces), onions and salt in stock pot (12 quart). Add water to within one inch of top.

❑ Place stock pot covered with lid on high heat. When it starts to boil, reduce heat to maintain a boil, but not so vigorous that it spills out the top. After it has boiled down so about 4 inches of water remain, fill with cold water to within 1 inch of top and continue to boil until 3 inches of "stock" remain. This takes about 1½ hours.

❑ Place a strainer over a large bowl and pour the "stock" into the bowl.

❑ Remove meat from the strainer and carcass. Cut into small pieces (or break with fingers after it cools). Add to stock.

❑ Put stock, meat, pepper, parsley, bouillon cubes, potato and food coloring in stock pot and fill with water. Bring to boil and maintain the boil with reduced heat for 30 minutes.

❑ Add noodles. Fill with cold water and boil until noodles are soft.

☞ This recipe creates about 10 quarts of soup. The remaining portion can be divided and packaged into containers and frozen for several months. Most soups are considered an appetizer; however, this soup is considered a meal in itself.

Vegetables

RANCH STYLE BEANS

½	pound bacon	½	pound hamburger
3	large onions, sliced	½	cup cider vinegar
¾	cup brown sugar	1	teaspoon dry mustard
½	teaspoon garlic powder	2	15-oz cans red kidney beans
4	15-oz cans baked beans	1	tablespoon vegetable oil

❒ Cook bacon and crumble. Set aside.

❒ Cook hamburger and onions in hot oil.

❒ Add bacon, hamburger and onions to crock pot.

❒ Add remainder of ingredients and cook several hours.

RICE PILAF

1 9-ounce box *Near East* brand rice pilaf

1 cube butter

❒ Follow directions on *Near East* box; but use 1 cube of butter instead of ½ cube.

SPICED REFRIED BEANS (FRIJOLES REFRITOS)

1 16-ounce can refried beans

2 green onions, chopped

2 chili poblano (canned, mild, green chilies), chopped

½ jalapeño chili, chopped (seeds are very hot, can be removed)

½ garlic clove, minced

⅛ chili piquene (very hot, small, dried red chili), chopped (optional)

❒ Mix together and cook in saucepan over medium heat until hot and bubbly. Stir occasionally.

☞ Wash your hands carefully after handling chilies, before accidentally rubbing your eyes.

Main Dishes

DAR'S FILLO BURRITOS

1 pound lean ground beef	¼ pound bacon
1 small onion — chopped	1 medium tomato — chopped
¾ teaspoon garlic powder	⅛ teaspoon Old Bay seasoning
¼ teaspoon oregano	¼ teaspoon chili powder
8 ounces bean dip	Fillo dough
½ cube butter — melted	Monterey jack cheese

❏ Cook bacon until crisp. Dice when cool.

❏ Cook ground beef, drain off fat and crumble.

❏ Blend burrito mixture together: onion, tomato, garlic powder, Old Bay, oregano, chili powder, bean dip, bacon and hamburger.

❏ Cut fillo dough into 3-inch strips and lay a double thickness onto a damp towel. Brush with melted butter.

❏ Place small tablespoon of burrito mixture on end of fillo dough and cover with a piece of Monterey jack cheese.

❏ Fold into a triangle and place in a casserole dish.

❏ Bake at 325° for 25 minutes.

☞ Cook the bacon on medium heat. Remove bacon and place the strips on a paper towel before it appears to be done. Check it after a couple of minutes, it's probably just right. Many cooks tend to overcook bacon.

When frying bacon, dip the bacon strips in cold water before frying. This will keep them from curling up.

CHICKEN CORDON BLEU

6	chicken breasts, skinned, boned
1	8-ounce package Swiss cheese slices
1	8-ounce package sliced cooked ham
3	tablespoons all-purpose flour
1	teaspoon paprika
6	tablespoons butter
½	cup dry white wine
1	chicken-flavor bouillon cube (or envelope)
1	tablespoon cornstarch
1	cup heavy cream (or whipping cream)

☐ Spread chicken breasts flat. Fold cheese and ham slices to fit on top. Fold breasts over filling and fasten edges with toothpicks.

☐ On waxed paper, mix flour and paprika. Coat chicken pieces with this mixture.

☐ Add butter to skillet over medium heat and cook chicken until browned on all sides. Add wine and bouillon. Reduce heat, cover and simmer 30 minutes or until fork-tender. Remove toothpicks.

☐ Blend cornstarch and cream until smooth and gradually stir into another skillet. Cook, stirring constantly, until thickened. Serve over chicken.

CHILI

2	tablespoons oil	1	bay leaf
2	garlic cloves—minced	½	teaspoon cayenne pepper
2	med onions—chopped	½	teaspoon powdered mustard
3	lbs lean ground beef	¼	teaspoon Tabasco sauce
½	teaspoon salt	1	teaspoon ground cumin
¼	teaspoon black pepper	2	tablespoons white vinegar
1	teaspoon paprika	2	six ounce cans tomato paste
2	tablespoons chili powder	¼	teaspoon oregano
1	15-oz can tomato sauce	1	jalapeño pepper—chopped
2	30-oz cans chili beans (optional)		
1	12-ounce jar La Victoria Salsa Suprema		
2	tablespoons green bell pepper — chopped		
1	28-oz can peeled tomatoes-sliced		

- ❐ Cook the garlic and onions in oil until golden brown. Add ground beef and brown. Stir in salt and pepper.
- ❐ In a stock pot or crock pot, add beef ingredients to 1 pint (2 cups) water.
- ❐ Add remaining ingredients and simmer 4 hours.
- ❐ Serve piping hot with garlic bread.

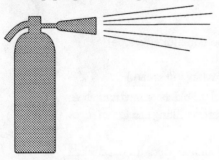 

GREEN CHILI (CHILI VERDE)

MEAT

2½ lbs shoulder pork roast	¾ pounds pork soup bones
1½ teaspoons Old Bay Seasoning	

SAUCE

2 8-oz. tomato sauce	1 6-oz. tomato paste
3 16-oz. canned tomatoes — strained and chopped	
1¼ tbsp. garlic powder	3½ cups hot water

SPICES

3 7-oz. can Oretega diced green chili strips

1 oz. Ortega diced hot peppers

1 tablespoon sugar	1 tablespoon salt

- ❐ Cut pork roast into ¼- to ½-inch squares. Place pork bones and pork in frying pan. Sprinkle with *Old Bay* seasoning. Cook over low heat until browned.
- ❐ Add sauce ingredients to meat ingredients and bring to rapid boil. Boil for 30 minutes.
- ❐ Add spices and continue boiling 20-30 minutes. Then cook on medium heat for 1 hour.
- ❐ Remove bones.

TETON APPLE CIDER-BAKED HAM

1   5- to 7-pound fully cooked ham, rump half
4   cups apple cider (apple juice)
2   medium onions, quartered

2	tablespoons lemon juice	1	beaten egg
⅓	cup packed brown sugar	1	teaspoon ground cloves

☐ Preheat oven to 325°.

☐ Combine apple cider (or apple juice), onions, and 2 tablespoons lemon juice in roasting pan.

☐ Place ham, fat side up, in shallow roasting pan. Score in diamonds on top surface (make diagonal ¼-inch-deep cuts across ham, first in one direction, then the other to form a diamond pattern).

☐ Bake in 325° oven for 1¾ hours (30 minutes for each pound).

☐ Brush the top surface of the ham with the beaten egg. Combine brown sugar and ground cloves and pat onto the egg (top surface of the ham). If you use a thermometer, insert meat thermometer at this time, making sure tip does not rest on bone or fat (not really necessary unless you use a country-style ham). Return ham to oven.

☐ Continue baking for 30 minutes or until thermometer registers 140°, basting ham each 10 minutes, be careful not to wash off all the brown sugar with the cider mixture. Remove from oven.

☐ Transfer ham to serving platter. To carve ham, place cut side down on cutting board. Cut along bone from top to board to remove a large boneless piece. Place this boneless piece of ham cut side down on the cutting board and slice meat across the grain. To carve meat remaining on the bone, make horizontal slices.

Country-style hams are specially processed to give them a distinctive flavor. They are dry-salt cured, sometimes smoked, and usually aged. They have not been completely cooked during processing. Bake them to an internal temperature of 160°. Follow label directions for scrubbing and soaking these hams.

☞ The apple cider and onions will draw the salt out of the ham and impart a fantastic flavor.

DELLA'S BAKED HAM

1   ham roast
1   tablespoons powdered mustard
1½ cups brown sugar
3   tablespoons pineapple juice
15 whole cloves
4   Maraschino cherries
½ cup champagne (optional)
    pineapple slices

☐ Preheat over to 325°. Place ham in casserole dish and bake 30 minutes for each pound. *Make several ¼-inch cuts along the length of the ham to retain the juices and basting ingredients.*

☐ Mix mustard, brown sugar and pineapple juice in bowl.

☐ With 45-minutes cooking time remaining, brush mixture of mustard, sugar and juice all over the top and sides of the ham to form a glaze. Push cloves into the ham with equal spacing.

☐ With 10 minutes cooking time remaining, brush champagne over ham.

☐ After slicing, garnish with pineapple slices and cherries.

☐ Serve hot.

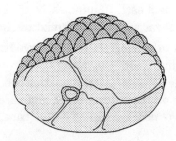

To elimiate odors from the refrigerator for a month or two, place an open box of baking soda on a back shelf. To kill any mildew fungus, wash the inside of the refrigerator with vinegar and let the acid do its work.

UNCLE RON'S JAMBALAYA

1	lb medium-size shrimps		
3	chicken breasts (boneless, skinless)		
½	pound cooked ham	24	large shucked oysters
4	tablespoons butter	2	tablespoons salad oil
¾	cup green pepper, diced	⅓	cup onions, minced
1	teaspoon garlic, minced	1	bay leaf, minced
¼	teaspoon thyme	¼	teaspoon saffron
¼	teaspoon ground cloves	¼	teaspoon ground allspice
1½	cups long-grain rice	4	large tomatoes, peeled, diced
1	tbsp. parsley, minced	¼	teaspoon Tabasco sauce
2	tablespoons lemon juice		salt
	pepper		

❒ Add 1 quart cold water and ½ teaspoon salt to a pot with shrimps. Slowly bring to a boil. Reserve liquid, peel and devein shrimps.

❒ Dice chicken and ham. Place in large Dutch oven with oil and 2 tablespoons butter. Sauté until chicken loses raw color.

❒ Add green pepper, onions, garlic, bay leaf and thyme. Sauté until onions lose color.

❒ Add 3½ cups shrimp stock (add water if necessary), saffron, ground cloves, allspice, rice, tomatoes, parsley, Tabasco sauce, lemon juice, 1 teaspoon salt and ½ teaspoon pepper.

❒ Mix well and bring to a boil. Reduce heat and simmer 20 minutes with a lid over the pot. Do not stir.

❒ Sauté oysters in 2 tablespoons butter until edges begin to curl.

❒ Add oysters and shrimp. Cook until rice is not too moist.

FANTASTIC OMELET

sausage—cooked and crumbled
green pepper — chopped fine

3 whole eggs	tomato — chopped
¼ teaspoon salt	mushrooms — sliced thin
¼ teaspoon pepper	cheese — grated
⅛ teaspoon oregano	pinch parsley flakes
1 tablespoon water	green onions — sliced thin
1 tablespoon butter	pinch of cornstarch

❑ Cook sausage, drain fat and crumble.

❑ Since an omelet is made rapidly, prepare and then combine ingredients in a bowl (include sausage).

❑ Place eggs, salt, pepper, cornstarch (makes the omelet fluffier), oregano and 1 tablespoon water in a bowl. Beat with a fork until well mixed.

❑ Place 1 tablespoon butter in frying pan on high heat until the butter turns hazelnut in color.

❑ Pour egg mixture in pan.

❑ When egg mixture coagulates, pour stuffing onto eggs on the half away from the pan handle.

❑ Tilt the pan up and use the flat side of a fork or spatula to start folding the edges back and over the stuffing, shaping it into a half-moon shape.

☞ This is a great dish in which to get rid of leftovers. Crumble a hamburger, add bacon and ham, various kinds of cheese, dice a left over onion.

To remove spots from stainless steel stove tops or sinks, use a cloth dampened with clob soda or white vinegar or rubbing alcohol.

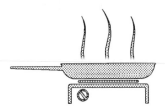
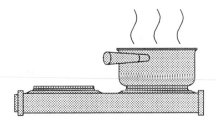

SPAGHETTI SAUCE

2	onions, thinly sliced	1	stick celery, chopped
½	green pepper, chopped	3	garlic cloves, minced

☐ Sauté in 1 tablespoon olive oil until the onions are soft.

2	pounds country sausage	4	pounds lean ground beef
1½	tablespoons fennel seeds		

☐ Sauté in olive oil until the meat is cooked.

2	6-oz cans tomato paste	5	8-ounce cans tomato sauce
1	6-ounce can V-8 juice	1	15-oz can Italian tomato sauce
3	large tomatoes, diced	1	tbsp. coarse black pepper
3	bay leaves	3	tablespoons oregano
1	tablespoon tarragon	½	teaspoon garlic powder
½	ounce Italian seasoning	3	tbsp. Worcestershire sauce
20	sliced stuffed green olives	2	tsp. Durkee RedHot Sauce
2	teaspoons celery salt	3½	tbsp. beef instant bouillon
1	cup red wine (Lambrusco—see Wines For Cooking, p. 64)		

☐ Add all ingredients to a stock pot or crock pot and cook several hours on medium heat.

☐ Serve over spaghetti.

BARBECUE SALMON (WHOLE)

1	3- to 5-lb dressed salmon	¼	cup chopped green onion
¼	cup chopped parsley	¼	cup butter
⅛	teaspoon pepper	½	cup mushrooms, sliced
1	9-ounce box Near East brand rice pilaf		

☐ In a saucepan, cook the *Near East* rice pilaf according to directions, except add 1 cube of butter instead of ½ cube.

(Continued)

❐ When rice is done, add chopped parsley, green onion, pepper and mushrooms.

❐ Sit dressed salmon on a sheet of aluminum foil. Stuff with rice mixture and cover with another sheet of aluminum foil. Wrap foil tight.

❐ Cook at medium temperature on barbecue grill for 15-20 minutes per pound (fish should flake easily with fork).

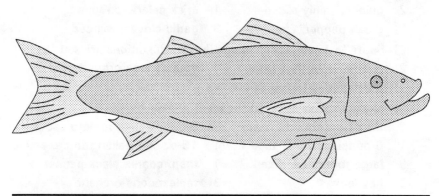

BARBECUE GRILLED SALMON STEAKS

4   fresh or frozen salmon steaks
⅓   cup cooking oil
3   tablespoons lemon juice   1   teaspoon dried dillweed
2   tbsp. parsley, chopped   ¼   teaspoon salt
¼   teaspoon dry mustard   dash pepper

❐ Combine oil, lemon juice, dillweed, parsley, salt, dry mustard and pepper in a shallow pan or bowl.

❐ Marinate salmon steaks for 1-2 hours at room temperature.

❐ Grill steaks for 5-8 minutes, basting often with marinade.

❐ Turn steaks and continue cooking for another 5-8 minutes, basting with marinade mixture.

❐ Steaks are done when fish flakes easily with a fork.

Place frozen fish in a pan of milk to thaw.
This imparts a fresh-caught flavor.

BROILED STEAKS

New York cut steaks
Mountain Man Barbecue Sauce
Bacon

❐ Skewer bacon strips around the edges of the steak.

❐ Brown steaks on barbecue grill on each side using medium heat, basting frequently with barbecue sauce.

❐ Cook as desired (rare, medium or well done) on low heat, continuing to baste with sauce.

❐ Serve sizzling hot.

☞See **Cooking Time for Meats**, page 50, to determine the time to cook various thickness cuts.

CRAB AND SHRIMP CASSEROLE

1	cup mayonnaise	1	6–8 oz. canned crab meat
1	6–8 oz. canned shrimp	8	ounces canned milk
5	hardboiled eggs–sliced	2	tbsp. onion–chopped
2	tbsp. parsley–chopped	1	cup soft bread crumbs
1	tsp. coarse black pepper	½	teaspoon salt
2	cups bread crumbs		

❐ Mix together all ingredients except 2 cups bread crumbs in casserole dish.

❐ Sprinkle 2 cups bread crumbs over the top.

❐ Bake in preheated oven at 300° for 35-40 minutes.

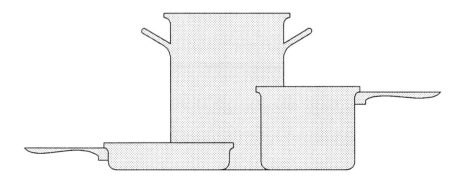

Condiments, Seasonings and Sauces

BARBECUE SAUCE

½ cup soy sauce	½ cup catsup
¼ tsp. Durkee RedHot	1 tbsp. Worcestershire sauce
¼ cup red wine vinegar	¾ cup water
1 tablespoon sugar	1 teaspoon salt
1 teaspoon celery seed	1 tablespoon brown sugar
juice of 1 lemon	¼ cup pineapple juice
1 medium onion, diced	1 teaspoon chili powder
¼ teaspoon dry mustard	1 tablespoon salad oil
½ teaspoon sweet basil	1 tablespoon dark corn syrup
1 16-oz can tomato paste	1 tablespoon corn starch
½ teaspoon pepper	1 garlic clove, minced

❑ Combine ingredients in a saucepan and bring to a boil.
❑ Reduce heat and simmer 15 minutes.

☞ Use this mixture to marinate and baste pork loins, steaks and baby back ribs. If you cook with a very hot grill, you might want to wait until the last 10 minutes of cooking before basting with this sauce so it doesn't burn.

SPARKY'S BLEU CHEESE (ROQUEFORT) DRESSING

1 pint mayonnaise	½ pint buttermilk
5 tablespoons sugar	¼ cup olive oil
¼ cup vinegar	4 ounces sour cream
1 egg	½ tablespoon lemon juice
Juice from 8 ounce can of pineapple chunks	
Bleu cheese	

❑ Mix all ingredients except bleu cheese together.
❑ Stir in crumbled bleu cheese to taste.

ROQUEFORT DRESSING

1	quart mayonnaise	1	cup buttermilk
1	tablespoon MSG	4	tablespoons steak sauce
½	tablespoon A-1	½	lemon
1	tablespoon garlic powder	⅓	tablespoon Worcestershire
15	ounces Roquefort Cheese		

☐ Mix ingredients.

GARLIC BUTTER

Soak 3 garlic cloves in 3 cups of boiling water for 5-minutes. Remove the cloves and pound to a pulp. Cream in one cube of butter. *In addition to using this on French bread, it makes a fine topping on a sizzling steak.*

GARLIC OIL

This is impossible to purchase in some areas, but simple to make. Obtain a jar with a cork or locking lid (½- to 1-pint size). Place 4 lemon peels, 4 pitted black olives and 4 shelled garlic cloves on a wooden skewer (alternating, if desired). Place skewer in jar and fill with olive oil (1 cup for ½ pint) and place it in the cupboard for one week before using.

SWEET HOT HOMEMADE MUSTARD

½ cup sifted all-purpose flour
¼ cup sugar
⅛ teaspoon salt
½ cup dry mustard (¼ cup if you like it less hot)
¾ cup cider vinegar
  Pinch of tumeric (for color)

☐ Mix dry ingredients and vinegar and blend to a velvety smoothness. Let stand in mustard jar for several days to season before using.

MOUNTAIN MAN BARBECUE SAUCE

3	garlic cloves, chopped	2	tbsp. Worcestershire sauce
2	onions, quartered	1	lemon
1	cup oil	2	jalapeño peppers
2	cups vinegar	1½	teaspoon powdered mustard
1	teaspoon salt	2	pinches parsley flakes
1	teaspoon black pepper	1	can beer (optional)

❑ Roll a lemon back and forth using pressure from the palm of the hand to break it down. Slice in half across the middle. Squeeze the juice from both halves into a saucepan. Don't worry about the seeds, but if you do: *Use cheese cloth or thin cloth around the lemon to catch the seeds.*

❑ Combine all the remaining ingredients, including one half of the lemon rind) into the saucepan.

❑ Place over high heat and bring to a boil. Reduce the heat and simmer for 30 minutes.

Try this, Pilgrim!

☞ This sauce is different than the red sauce many of us associate with barbecue sauces, but don't neglect to try it because of this. It adds a distinct flavor to barbecued pork ribs, chicken and steaks.

MEXICAN SALSA

6	ripe tomatoes	3	large onions
1	4-ounce can green chilies	½	cup celery
¼	cup green pepper	½	teaspoon mustard seed
2	tbsp. red wine vinegar	¼	cup olive oil
½	teaspoon cumin	½	teaspoon oregano
1	tsp. salt & ½ tsp. pepper	1	tbsp. green onion, minced
1	tbsp. parsley, chopped	1	tablespoon cilantro, chopped
½	tsp. ground coriander	1	tsp. lemon juice

❑ Mince tomatoes, onions, chilies, celery and green pepper.

❑ Add remainder of ingredients and mix well.

❑ Refrigerate several hours to let flavors blend.

MIGUEL'S PICO DE GALLO (Beak of the Rooster) or SALSA FRESCA (Fresh Salsa)

2	med tomatoes, chopped	4	green onions, chopped
1	serrano chili, chop fine	1½	teaspoons cilantro, chopped
	juice of 1 lime	½	clove garlic, minced
1	tsp. olive oil	⅙	cup cold water
1	jalapeño chili, minced		

❒ Mix all ingredients in a bowl with the juice of the tomatoes.

❒ Chill for 2 hours to let the spices mix.

❒ Serve with fajitas, omelets, fish or tostada chips.

CILANTRO is the parsleylike leaves of fresh coriander. Be careful with the Serrano chili. Although small, it is really hot. Wash your hands carefully after handling the chili so you don't get any in your eyes by accidentally rubbing them.

SHRIMP COCKTAIL SAUCE

½	cup tomato ketchup		
½	tsp. lemon juice (fresh or concentrate)		
1	rounded tsp. horseradish	1	teaspoon brandy (optional)
½	tsp. Worcestershire sauce	½	teaspoon parsley flakes
	dash of salt		dash of sugar

❒ Put all ingredients in a bowl and blend. Top with additional small amount of parsley flakes.

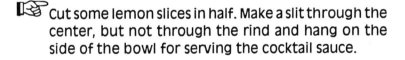 Cut some lemon slices in half. Make a slit through the center, but not through the rind and hang on the side of the bowl for serving the cocktail sauce.

> If you use canned shrimp for salads, you can eliminate the "canned" taste by soaking the shrimp for about 15 minutes in a mixture of 2 tablespoons Sauterne or dry vermouth and 2 tablespoons vinegar, then rinse.

Breads

SOUR DOUGH BREAD

STARTER

1 package dry yeast	2 cups warm water
2 cups unbleached flour	

- ☐ Place yeast in mixing bowl and stir in water.
- ☐ Add flour and blend.
- ☐ Cover with a shower cap (the kind provided by motels) or plastic wrap and let stand at room temperature for 48-hours.
- ☐ Store starter in refrigerator in a bowl with a loose-fitted lid.

STARTER MAINTENANCE

1 cup unbleached flour	1 cup milk
⅓ cup sugar	Starter

- ☐ Each time some of the starter is removed to make bread or pancakes, it must be replaced.
- ☐ Each week, even if the starter has not been used, mix together the starter with flour, milk and sugar.

BREAD

1 package dry yeast	¼ cup warm water
1 teaspoon sugar	1 egg
¼ cup vegetable oil	½ cup water
1 teaspoon salt	⅓ cup sugar
1 cup sourdough starter	3½ cups flour

- ☐ In a jar with a lid, mix the yeast and warm water. Shake until the yeast is dissolved.
- ☐ In a bowl, mix the egg, vegetable oil, water, salt and sugar.
- ☐ Add the yeast mixture and sourdough starter.
- ☐ Blend in two cups of the flour while mixing thoroughly (wooden spoon or electric mixer). Add remaining 1½ cups flour and mix with wooden spoon.
- ☐ Turn out onto a floured surface and knead (using a folding-back and pressing-forward motion) to a consistent mixture. If it remains sticky, add additional flour.

(Continued)

- ☐ Place a baggie or plastic bag over hand and wipe mixing bowl with thin coating of vegetable oil.
- ☐ Place dough in bowl and turn until dough is covered with oil.
- ☐ Cover with cloth and let rise in warm place until double in bulk, about 2 hours.
- ☐ Punch down and knead again (on floured surface) for 2-3 minutes.
- ☐ Cut in half and place in well-greased loaf pans. Cover and let rise in warm place for 2 hours.
- ☐ Bake at 350° for 20-25 minutes, until top is golden brown.

While I was growing up my folks stressed that breakfast was the most important meal. We always had sourdough pancakes and elk steaks or elk steaks with sourdough biscuits and gravy. Sourdough is a pain to maintain, but if you like it, it's worth the trouble.

CROISSANTS
YEAST BATTER

2	packages dry yeast	¾	cup evaporated milk
1	cup warm water	1½	teaspoons salt
1	egg	⅓	cup sugar
¼	cup melted butter		

FLOUR MIXTURE
1 cup chilled butter
5 cups unsifted flour

EGG AND WATER MIXTURE
1 egg beaten with 1 tablespoons water

- ☐ Place warm water in a bowl. Sprinkle yeast over water.
- ☐ Stir in 1 cup flour, evaporated milk, salt, egg, sugar, and melted butter.
- ☐ Beat until smooth and set aside.
- ☐ In a large bowl, place 4 cups flour. Cut in chilled butter until butter particles are bean sized.
- ☐ Pour yeast mixture over flour mixture. Use a spatula to turn the mixture until all the flour is moistened.

(Continued)

❐ Cover bowl with shower cap (or plastic wrap) and refrigerate 4-5 hours.

❐ Place dough on floured surface and punch down. Knead several times to release air bubbles.

❐ Cut dough into 4 parts. Roll dough on floured surface into pie shape and cut into 8 pie-shaped wedges.

❐ Roll wedges from outside edge toward center and leave the point under.

❐ Place on ungreased cookie sheet and turn edges to form a crescent shape. Allow 1-2 inches between each croissant.

❐ Cover with cloth until double in size. Brush with egg-water mixture.

❐ Bake in preheated oven at 400° for 12-15 minutes.

REFRIGERATOR DINNER ROLLS

2	yeast cakes	½ cup lukewarm water
1	tablespoon sugar	

❐ Dissolve yeast in water with sugar and set aside.

1	cup milk—scalded	2	eggs
¼	cup shortning	4	cups flour
½	cup sugar	2	teaspoons salt

❐ Add the sugar and shortning to the hot milk.

❐ When cool, add salt to beaten eggs.

❐ Add eggs and flour to milk mixture.

❐ Beat and set aside to rise. Punch down and shape as desired. Let it rise and bake in preheated oven at 350° for 15 to 20 minutes.

❐ If kept in the fridge (covered) overnight or for a few days, shape and let rise 1 time then bake in preheated oven at 350° for 15 to 20 minutes.

☞ Roll dough into pie shape. Cut into triangular shape. Roll from outside edge toward center. Allow 1 inch between each roll.

Desserts

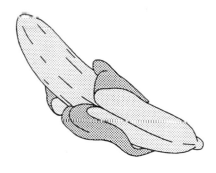
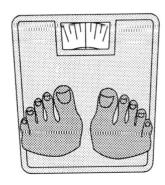

BANANAS FLAMBÉ

3	tablespoons butter
1	cup brown sugar
	orange peel
	brandy
	white rum
	banana liqueur
4	dashes ground cloves (½ teaspoon)
4	dashes ground cinnamon
6	peeled ripe bananas, cut in half lengthwise
	vanilla ice cream

☐ Melt butter in medium skillet.

☐ Add brown sugar and carmelize (heat dry sugar over low heat to a liquid state until it becomes a golden brown. Move the pan on and off the heat source to keep from burning). While cooking, add orange zest (grate peel).

☐ Add 1 ounce each of brandy, white rum and banana liqueur and ignite.

☐ Add bananas and cook until lightly browned. Turn once.

☐ Serve the bananas with ice cream and spoon the sauce over.

I jotted this recipe down while watching it being made at Hector's Restaurant, in the LaPosada Motel, Laredo, Texas.

CHERRIES JUBILEE

2 tablespoons butter	½ cup white sugar
Orange peel	Cherry liqueur

2 cups canned dark sweet cherries, drained
Vanilla ice cream

- ☐ Melt butter in medium skillet.
- ☐ Add sugar and carmelize (heat dry sugar over low heat to a liquid state until it becomes a golden brown. Move the pan on and off the heat source to keep from burning). Add orange zest (grate peel).
- ☐ Add cherries and ¾ cup cherry liqueur and ignite with long match. Let burn until flames die.
- ☐ Spoon hot cherries and sauce over ice cream.

CHOCOLATE CHIP AND NUT COOKIES

CREAM TOGETHER:

2 cups butter	2 cups sugar
2 cups brown sugar	

ADD:

4 eggs	2 teaspoons vanilla

MIX TOGETHER:

5 cups oatmeal (small amounts in blender til turned to powder)	
4 cups flour	1 teaspoon salt
2 teaspoons baking powder	2 teaspoons baking soda

ADD:

1 24 oz pkg chocolate chips	1 8 ounce Hershey Bar, grated
3 cups chopped nuts, any kind (walnuts, macadamias, etc.)	

- ☐ Bake on ungreased cookie sheet. Make golf ball sized cookies, two inches apart. Bake at 375° for 6 minutes. Makes 9 dozen cookies.

MOM'S PIE DOUGH

4 cups all-purpose flour

1	tablespoon sugar	2	tablespoons salt
1	cup shortening	¾	cups butter
½	cup water	1	egg
2	tablespoons cider vinegar (makes crust extra flaky)		

☞ If using self-rising flour, omit the salt. Pastry made with self-rising flour differs in flavor and texture from that made with all-purpose flour. If desired, whole grain flour can be substituted for up to half of the all-purpose flour, adding a little more water if necessary.

❏ Place the flour (lightly spoon the flour into a measuring cup and level off with a knife), sugar and salt in a large bowl. Mix thoroughly before adding shortening, vinegar, egg (beat with fork) and butter. Mix (by hand, with pastry blender or with two knives used in scissor fashion) the ingredients enough so all the butter pieces are coated with flour (the mixture forms coarse crumbs).

❏ Add water. Sprinkle the mixture with water a tablespoon at a time, while tossing and mixing lightly with a fork. Do not use stirring motion as shortening will melt causing tough pastry. Start kneading the ingredients to gather the dough into a ball. Add water until dough is just moist enough to hold together (Too much water causes the dough to become sticky and tough; too little water causes edges to crack and pastry to tear easily while rolling). Do not worry if there are little pieces of plain butter here and there. This will give flakiness to the dough, making it slightly similar to a puff pastry. The dough should be malleable and usable right away. If overworked, it will become elastic, in which case you should let it "rest" in the refrigerator for 1 hour before using. If sticky, cover and chill at least 2 hours for easier handling.

☞ To prepare pastry in food processor: Place flour, salt and shortening in processor bowl. Process 20 to 30 seconds until mixture resembles coarse crumbs. With machine running, add minimum amount of cold water all at once through feed tube. Process 20 to 30 seconds or just until ball forms. If ball does not form in 30 seconds, shape into ball with hands. Wrap dough in plastic wrap and refrigerate 30 minutes or freeze 10 minutes before continuing as directed above.

☞ LOW ALTITUDE — Below 3,500 feet: When preparing pastry in food processor, decrease water by 2 table-spoons.

☞ Although pie dough is easier to make with a combi-nation of butter and shortening, an all-butter dough is finer. When working with dough, remem-ber the more you knead and the more water you use, the more elasticity and shrinkage you get. The less water and the more fat you use, the more crumbly and lax the dough will be. At one end of the spectrum you have the bread dough (flour and water) which is elastic, springy and unrollable. At the other end, the cookie dough (mainly flour and fat) is soft, crumbly and hard to roll. The pie dough is in the middle and will lean toward one side or the other, depending on ingredients and method.

ROLLING AND FORMING PIE DOUGH

❐ Place the dough on a floured board and roll it uniformly to obtain a consistent ⅛-inch thickness. While rolling, turn the dough a quarter turn after each few strokes to obtain a round wheel shape.

❐ Lift the edge of the dough onto the rolling pin and roll it back on the pin. Lift it up and unroll it over the 9-inch pan (metal or glass).

- ❏ Push the dough into the corners of the pan so it doesn't shrink during baking.
- ❏ Holding your fingers against the inside edge of the pan against the dough, pull a ½-inch portion of the dough back into the pan.
- ❏ Use a knife or roll the rolling pin across the top of the pie pan to cut off the excess dough. This excess dough may be refrigerated for about three days before further use (make some tarts, fill with jam, crimp and bake) or it may be frozen about three months.
- ❏ If you are making an open top pie, e.g. pumpkin pie, form a border along the edge of the pan with your fingers (pinch the dough between your thumb and forefinger every ½-inch), the tines of a fork or a dough crimper.
- ❏ The shell is now ready for the filling.
- ❏ If the pie has dough on top of the filling, pinch the top and bottom layers together with your thumb and forefinger.

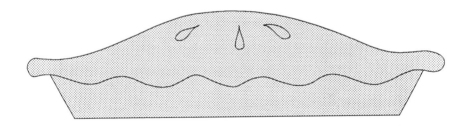

CHERRY PIE

1   20-ounce can Cherry Pie Filling

- ❏ Make pie dough as described above.
- ❏ Mix and spread on bottom of crust with fingers ---- 1 tablespoon flour and 2 tablespoons sugar.
- ❏ Add the pie filling.
- ❏ Add ¼ cup water to the cherry pie filling can and pour it on top of the filling. Cut four butter patties and place on top of the filling. Add top pie crust and brush with milk (enough to get the sugar to stick) and sprinkle with sugar. Bake at 375°- 400° for ½- to ¾-hour.

POTICA BREAD (YUGOSLAVIAN NUT ROLL)

Preparation time: 3 hours   Cooking time: 40 minutes

DOUGH:

1   cup milk — heated
½   cup granulated sugar
1   teaspoon salt
¼   cup butter
1½ tbsp. honey
2   pkg. active dry yeast
¼   cup water, 110°
2   eggs
4½ cups all-purpose flour

FILLING:

4   c. (1 lb.) walnuts, chop fine
3   ounces pecans, chopped fine
3   eggs, slightly beaten
1   cup brown sugar, packed
1   tablespoon honey
⅛   cup butter, melted
1½ tsp. cinnamon, ground
1   teaspoon vanilla extract
3   tablespoons butter, melted

PROCEDURE FOR DOUGH:

☐ Heat 1 cup milk and stir in sugar, salt, butter and honey. Let cool to room temperature.

☐ In a large bowl, sprinkle 2 packages yeast over ¼ cup water heated to 110°. Stir to dissolve yeast; then stir in lukewarm milk mixture.

☐ Add eggs and 2½ cups flour. Beat at high speed with electric mixture for 2 minutes. Use a wooden spoon to beat in the remaining 2 cups flour.

☐ Knead dough with hands until it leaves sides of bowl. Place dough in large, lightly-greased bowl and turn to leave the greased side up. Cover with towel and let rise in warm place until double in bulk.

PROCEDURE FOR FILLING:

☐ Combine chopped nuts, eggs, brown sugar, honey, butter, cinnamon and vanilla extract in a bowl. Stir to blend well. Cover with towel until ready to fill loaves.

PREPARATION:

☐ After dough has doubled in bulk, punch it down. Scatter thin coating of flour on a board and turn dough out. Cover with bowl for 10 minutes.

- ❏ Cut dough in half. Use rolling pin to roll out dough until just over $1/16$-inch in thickness. Use $1/2$ filling and spread a thin coating all over to within $1/4$ inch from edge.
- ❏ Pick up the dough from the wide side and roll until a long roll with the seam down is formed. Hold one end and pull the other end around to form a coil or "U" shape. Place this on a greased baking sheet. Brush melted butter over dough.
- ❏ Roll out and fill the second loaf. Cover both with a towel and let rise for 1 hour.
- ❏ Preheat over to 350° and bake until the crust is golden brown (about 35-40 minutes).

RED WINE SAUCE

1   cup granulated sugar
$1/2$ cup water
$1/4$ cup red wine (claret or see **Wines for Cooking**, p. 64)
$1/4$ teaspoon grated lemon rind
      Vanilla ice cream

- ❏ Boil 1 cup sugar in $1/2$ cup water for 5 minutes. Cool.
- ❏ Add wine and lemon rind.
- ❏ Serve over vanilla ice cream.

BAKLAVA

My daughter, Lori, taught me to prepare this Turkish dessert.

Syrup

2   cups sugar
1   cup water
2   teaspoons lemon juice

- ❏ Combine sugar, water and lemon juice in pan. Bring to boil while stirring frequently.
- ❏ When mixture begins to boil, do not stir anymore.
- ❏ Cook 5 minues, remove and let cool.

(Continued)

Baklava

1   lb phyllo (filo, yufka) pastry sheets
1½ lbs ground or finely chopped nuts (walnuts and/or
     almonds (about 4 cups)
1½ cups butter, melted   ½ teaspoon ground allspice
½ cup sugar   ½ teaspoon cinnamon
½ teaspoon cloves   ½ cup dry bread crumbs

- ☐ Combine nuts, bread crumbs, sugar and spices in bowl and mix well.

- ☐ Brush bottom of large cookie sheet (11"x17" up to 14"x20") with butter and place about 10 pastry sheets on pan, brushing each sheet with butter.

- ☐ Sprinkle about 1 cup of the nut-spice mixture on top. Add another layer of about 10 pastry sheets, brushing each sheet with butter. Sprinkle another cup of the nut-spice mixture. Continue until the nut-spice mixture is gone.

- ☐ Reserve about 8 sheets for the top layer, brushing each sheet with butter.

- ☐ Make left and right diagonal cuts to form the baklava into diamond shapes.

- ☐ Sprinkle the top with water to prevent the pastry from curling up and bake for 1 hour at 300°F until golden brown (about 1 hour).

- ☐ Pour cool syrup over warm pastry and let stand several hours before serving.

MOM'S COCONUT DREAM BARS

CRUST

½ cup butter (soft)   ½ cup brown sugar
1   cup sifted flour

- ☐ Combine soft butter (room temperature), brown sugar and sifted flour in 8½" x 11" cake pan. Blend well with fingers.

- ☐ Press firmly into pan making edges ¼ to ⅜ inch higher so filling does not run over the edges.

- ☐ Bake at 325° for 10 minutes.

(Continued)

FILLING

⅛	teaspoon salt	1	cup brown sugar
1	teaspoon vanilla	2	tablespoons flour
½	teaspoon baking powder	1½	cups coconut
1	cup nuts - chopped	2	eggs - beaten

☐ Put ingredients in small bowl. Beat well; spread over baked crust. Bake about 20 minutes at 325° until meringue is brown.

If you have a leftover baked potato, you can use it again by rinsing in cold water, then baking for 20 minutes at 350°.

Cooking Time for Meats

BROILING MEATS

To broil steaks in an oven, check the manufacturer's recommendations. If there are no suggestions given, arrange the wire racks so the top of the steaks and chops of ¾ - to 1½ - inch-thick are about 3 inches from the heat. Thicker cuts of steaks and chops require the wire racks to be placed about 4 or 5 inches from the meat. Broil the meat on one side for about half the time listed, then turn over for the remainder of the time.

TIME TO COOK (MINUTES)

Beef Steaks	Rare	Medium	Well-done
1-inch	8-10	12-14	18-20
1½-inch	14-16	18-20	25-30
2-inch	20-25	30-35	40-45
Hamburgers	**Rare**	**Medium**	**Well-done**
½-inch	8	10	12
1-inch	15	20	25
Lamb Chops	**Rare**	**Medium**	**Well-done**
¾-inch	Not Applicable	10-12	13-15
1-inch	Not Applicable	11-13	16-18
1½-inch	Not Applicable	15-18	20-22

The following should be cooked for the amount of time listed:

Pork Chops	¾- to 1-inch	20-25
Pork Steaks	½- to ¾-inch	20-22
Ham Center Slice	½-inch	10-12
Fully cooked, bone-in	1-inch	16-18
Fish Fillets and	½- inch	5-6
Fish Steaks	1-inch	10-12

BAKING MEATS

When using a meat thermometer to determine when to remove the meat from the oven, insert the thermometer in meats so the bulb rests in the thickest part of the lean meat. For poultry, insert the thermometer in the middle of the inside thigh muscle. *Be certain the bulb does not rest in fat or touch bone* or an erroneous reading will be obtained.

Thermometer Reading for Removal from Oven

Beef

Rare	140°
Medium	160°
Well-done	170°
Veal	170°
Pork	170°

Ham

Fully Cooked	140°
Cook-before-eating	160°

Lamb

Rare	140°
Medium	160°
Well-done	170°-180°
Poultry	185°

Don't expose tomatoes to direct sunlight when trying to ripen them. The sunlight makes them soft.

Barbecue Grill Cooking Times

Barbecuing is as American as "Mom and apple pie." There is no better way to present colorful foods with excellent flavor and mouth-watering anticipation that with the use of an outdoor barbecue.

Barbecue equipment varies from charcoal brickettes to gas flame heated ceramic "briquets." The equipment you use doesn't matter as far as taste since it is the burning of fat that imparts the *barbecue* flavor to foods, not the charcoal or gas flame. The only difference the equipment makes is in the control of the temperature. With a gas-fired barbecue the temperature may be selected as *low, medium or high,* or any range inbetween. With a charcoal briquette barbecue, the food is moved closer or farther away from the coals to regulate temperature.

MEAT	CUT	PORTION	TIME (MINUTES) & TEMPERATURE
Roasts (tenderloin, eye round, rib, rump, chuck, blade or sirloin tip)	All sizes and shapes	1/3 to 1/2 pound (boneless) or 3/4 to 1 pound (bone in) per person	20-30 minutes per pound Low temperature
Steaks & Chops (Club, rib eye, porterhouse, sirloin fillet, T-bone)	1 to 1½ inch	1/2 to 3/4 pound per person	RARE--4-6 per side MEDIUM-7-10 per side WELL--9-12 per side Medium temperature
Steaks & Chops (Chuck, cross rib, round)	1 to 1½ inch	1/2 pound per person	RARE--5-7 per side MEDIUM--7-10 per side WELL - Not Recommended Medium temperature
Hamburger	Lean ground beef	1 pound makes 2 to 4 burgers	RARE--3 per side MEDIUM--5 per side WELL--7-10 per side Medium temperature
Chicken	Whole	1 pound per person	1 to 1½ hours Low temperature
Chicken	Pieces	3/4 to 1 pound per person	1 hour Low temperature

Leg of Lamb	Whole, boned or rolled	1 pound for 3 servings	30-35 per pound Low temperature
Spareribs	Loin back ribs Country-style ribs	1 pound per person 1 pound per person	30 to 1 hour, turn frequently 40-50 turn frequently Medium temperature
Fish (cod, fillets, salmon, snapper, sole, trout) Shrimp	All kinds	1 pound per 2 or 3 persons	8-15 per side; 15-20 per pound for whole fish. Done when fish flakes easily with fork. Shrimp 3-4 per side. Medium temperature

Notes:

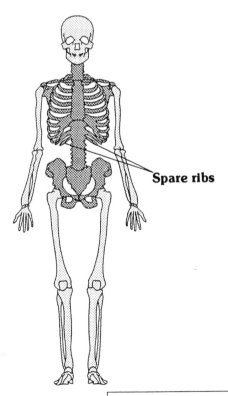

Spare ribs

Don't cry over onions---Refrigerate the onions before slicing, chopping or dicing and cut the root end last to eliminate tears.

Cooking Times for Breads, Etc.

BREADS	TEMPERATURE FAHRENHEIT	TIME MINUTES
Bread	400°	20
Corn Bread	400°	30
Fruit or nut bread	350°	60
Muffins	425°	20 to 30
Popovers	450° then 350°	20 then 15 to 20
Rolls	400-425°	14 to 20

CAKES

Angel Food	325-350°	50 to 75
Chocolate Layer	350°	25 to 35
Chocolate Square	350°	35 to 45
Cup	375°	20 to 25

COOKIES

Fruit or chocolate	325-350°	10 to 15
Drop or rolled	375-400°	8 to 12
Sliced refrigerator	400°	8 to 10

MERINGUES

Meringues	275°	45 to 60

PASTRY

Pie shells	450°	10 to 12
Puff pastry	450-500°	5 to 8
Tarts	450°	10 to 15

PIES

Deep-dish	450° then 350°	10 then 30 to 35
Meringues on cooked fillings	350°	10 to 15
One-crust	450° then 350°	10 then 25-30

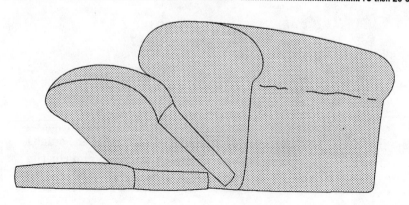

☞ PASTRY: When the temperature is too high, the crust may be too dark and the pie may not be evenly baked. When the temperature is too low, the crust may be pale and doughy and the filling may not be thoroughly cooked. If the pie is not baked long enough, the crust may be pale and the lower crust is doughy.

☞ CAKES: Cakes are baked when a toothpick inserted in the center comes out clean, the cake shrinks from the edges of the pan and the cake springs back when touched lightly with a finger.

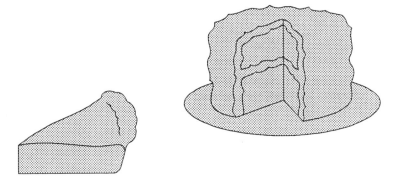

When frying or sautéing, place the frying pan on the stove and allow it to reach cooking temperature before adding the fats or oils (butter, margarine or cooking oil.) This eliminates all of the sticking and most of the spattering. A little salt will stop spattering.

Suggestions

EQUIPMENT

Most bachelor pads have some primitive ware, and a few lucky fellows may own a Microwave, electric mixer, a grill, food processor, dishwasher, etc. These are all great, but not absolutely necessary. Minimums you cannot get along without are:

Baking Sheet	Measuring Cups and Spoons
Can Opener	Chopping Board
Mixing Bowls	Knives (butcher, paring)
Coffee Pot	Mixing Spoons - wood
Egg Beater	Pie and Dessert Pans
Egg Whisk (wire whisk)	Rolling Pin
Flour Sifter	Salt & Pepper Shakers
Frying Pan(s)	Saucepan
Grater	Stock Pot (12 quart)
Knife Sharpener	Teapot

If you don't already have pots and pans, consider graniteware. It is dark, speckled enamel. There is no interaction with foods, it's inexpensive and it comes in many sizes.

Don't get carried away with gadgets. You'll find an electric can opener is just in your way, special egg cutters, tomato cutters, apple corers, machines to make radish roses and even electric knives just clutter your drawers, and really are not very useful. I've even found I can get along without a battery operated gadget that beats an egg while still in its shell.

SERVING

How the meal is served depends on the size of your cave and the furnishings. If you have a dining table, fine china, silver and crystal, you probably don't need this book. You can make do with what you have, serve the food with a flourish and never apologize. But, don't serve prime rib on paper plates or buffet style unless your provide TV trays or small tables for your guests. Card tables are a good solution or pick up a long folding table. You can even seat your guests on cushions around a large coffee table, if they are fairly agile. However, it is quite uncomfortable for your grandma with arthritis.

Put bread sticks in a clay flowerpot — that's taste. Chipped wine glasses—that's dowdy. More taste: If you inherited Grandma's old tin cream can, use it for ice cubes. If you have a big iron Dutch oven, fill it with soup and ladle it at the table. Baskets are versatile, beer bottles can hold candles—let the wax drip down the sides, and if it looks right use a coffee can for flowers. The container doesn't have to be used for its original purpose. To me, paper plates are vulgar and unrefined except for picnic type meals. Better to use unmatched plates. I like to serve coffee in a mug. If guests wander around sipping coffee, it's much easier to hold than a cup and saucer. A bachelor can get away with almost anything and be considered clever while a housewife might try the same thing and people would say "tsk, tsk, she should know better."

A cigarette dangling from your mouth as you cook—that's uncouth; a glass of wine at your elbow—that's polish. You'll know the difference. Good manners and being a good host are to make your guests comfortable in all ways.

DECORATIONS

A few sprigs of parsley add color to a platter, not to mention cherry tomatoes, halved if you wish, or bright pickled crab apples with pork. A bowl of fruit can always be used as a centerpiece and also may serve as dessert. Unconventional centerpieces are sometimes more effective than arranged carnations. Be different and set a trend.

SHOPPING FOR FOOD

Good ingredients are essential to a good finished product. If you don't want to splurge on steak, settle for lean ground round. Real butter makes a difference in the taste of many foods. In buying meat, if there is no waste $1/4$ to $1/8$ pound per person is sufficient. If there is some bone, allow $1/8$ to $1/2$ pound, and with bony cuts like spareribs, each guest can get away with one pound. Read the recipes beforehand and make a written list of everything you need.

GUESTS

Invite your friends. I have found that real estate people mix with pilots mix with ranchers mix with teachers mix with lawyers. A little contrast here is as important as with the food—something crunchy goes with something soft, something red or green adds interest to a dish whitish in color, something hot and something cold. Remember that bachelors are always in demand for dinner parties, and those who can cook are especially desirable. You will not have to cook many times before you find you're enjoying home cooking constantly.

LEFTOVERS

At the risk of raising the ire of some people, concerning leftovers— forget it; unless, of course, you luck out and have a slab of your prime rib left. I was always perplexed as a small child when my mother carefully stored everything left from a meal in the refrigerator. When she defrosted and cleaned it, she would dispose of many of those odds and ends as garbage. I never got a sensible answer when I asked "why?"

She always said it was sinful to waste food, when people in other countries were starving. (Also, I could never understand how I was helping the people in other countries by cleaning up my plate.) So, if you can't bear to throw it out, best get a big dog. Don't try to eat it and save it that way—better that it goes to waste than it goes to waist.

SALADS

Salads are fun and you'll find that you don't need a recipe. With a turkey soup or an oyster stew for a crowd, you might wish to set up a salad bar. In addition to a huge bowl of crisp greens, add your choice of onions and/or onion rings, radishes, sliced cauliflower, thin carrot and celery sticks, garbanzos, olives, mushrooms, pickled beets, bacos, sunflower nuts, chopped chives, croutons, grated or chunked cheese, hard boiled eggs, slivers of ham or turkey, cucumber slices, zucchini, marinated green beans and artichokes.

A variety of dressings can be placed alongside. Usually the dry mixes you shake up with milk or buttermilk and mayonnaise, or oil and vinegar are better than the bottled dressings.

Or toss it yourself, using whatever greens you like: lettuce, escarole, endive, spinach. Wash and shake dry and toss first with just a little garlic oil, then add whatever else is to your liking and toss with your choice of dressing just prior to serving.

A salad doesn't have to be tossed greens. Try grated raw carrots and chopped walnuts mixed with a little mayonnaise thinned with half and half and a sprinkle of sugar. Raisins can even be added.

Pare apples, core, and cook long and slowly in syrup made from cinnamon candies. When cold, fill the centers with cream cheese. Add some chopped pecans.

Parboil tomatoes for about one minute. Skin and stuff with cottage cheese mixed with a little cut chives and dust lightly with thyme.

Soak prunes until soft. Pit and stuff with cottage cheese and walnuts.

Believe it or not, apples and onion slices are compatible.

Cut red apples (unpeeled) into thin slices (remove the core first). Arrange some very thin slices of raw carrot on top and heap minced dates and nuts in the center. Serve with sour cream dressing.

Serve asparagus on a slice of beet with a dressing made with one cup mayonnaise, 2 tablespoons chili sauce, 2 tablespoons catsup and 2 teaspoons Worcestershire sauce.

Use fresh or canned pears. Roll 6 ginger snaps fine and mix with a 3-ounce package of cream cheese. Fill the cavity of the pear and serve with French dressing.

There are no set rules for salads and the combinations are endless.

DESSERTS

Desserts are superfluous after most of these dinners, but included are some of my favorites in case you do want to go all the way. Cherries Jubilee sounds and looks difficult (but not really). It is spectacular and will provide a dramatic finale to your perfect dinner.

A couple of tablespoons of Cointreau or Kirsch poured over freshly peeled fruit cut bite size make a lovely dessert after a rich meal. Use any or a combination of the following: oranges, bananas, white seedless grapes, apple, kiwi, pineapple, strawberries, peaches or raspberries.

Ice cream with 1½ tablespoons creme de menthe poured over it makes a refreshing ending. Top with a maraschino cherry for extra color.

Likewise, a red wine sauce shows sophistication (see index to make).

TABLE SETTING

LINEN - The bachelor has far more flexibility than the housewife in setting his table. Tablecloths may or may not be used and are available in fabric or plastic. Place mats take the place of tablecloths in most situations since they are less expensive and easier to take care of. Also, they help get rid of a "bare-table" effect.

PLATES and SILVERWARE - I think it's rather pretentious for a bachelor to go all out with a formal service using a service plate, dinner plate, entrée plate, dessert plate, bread-and-butter plate, soup plate, cream soup cup, bouillon cup, and after-dinner coffee cup and saucer. Can you image the dish washing involved? Instead, your entertaining should concentrate on a basic table setting. Whether formal or informal, the silver is laid out the same allowing for a sequential use starting with the outside utensil and working in toward the plate.

The bottom of the silverware parallels the base of the plate. The

cutting edge of the knife is toward the plate. The water glass is placed above the knife tip. Forks go to the left (except a cocktail fork which goes on the far right), the knife and spoons go to the right.

Using The Knife

When you cook, you use a knife. Bachelors have been exposed to knives since early boyhood, so there's no problem involving safety . . . just remember it's easier to get cut with a dull knife than a sharp knife. A few hints will make handling the knife easier, more productive and cooking more enjoyable.

PROPER TECHNIQUE - To chop, dice, mince or slice meats and vegetables, the item should be held with curled fingertips, keeping the second joint of the fingers in a vertical position. The knife blade is then abutted up against this second joint. The knife is continually held up against the second joints of the fingers. Moving the hand that holds the item will gauge the cut (controls the thickness of each slice). This is called the "curled finger technique."

CHOP GARLIC - Remove the skin or shell from an individual garlic clove and cut off the stem. Use the side of the knife blade with pressure from the palm to crush the clove. The remaining flesh is then chopped to the desired consistency.

CHOP - Hold the knife firmly by the handle with one hand and place the fingers of the other hand on top of the blade near the tip keeping the fingers straight. Rock the blade back and forth from the tip to the heel, occasionally scrape the pieces together into a pile.

CHOP PARSLEY - Bunch the parsley into a tight ball using the curled fingertip technique. Start slicing back and forth letting small portions of the parsley escape from your grip into the path of the knife blade. Next use the chopping technique.

DICE AN ONION - Cut onion in half lengthwise (from the stem to the tip) and peel it. Place onion on its flat side and make some horizontal slices of the desired thickness. Next, make vertical slices along the length, but don't cut all the way through the onion. Vertical slices across the width and all the way through completes the operation.

MINCE AN ONION - Follow the same technique as that outlined in "dice an onion," but make all slices of smaller thickness.

SLICE A POTATO - Hold the potato on its flattest side with the curled fingertip technique. If the potato has a tendency to move around, make a small slice to create a flat side which is turned down on the chopping block. Make vertical slices controlling the thickness with the movement of the curled fingertips rather than by moving the knife.

Shopping Quantity Calculator

Beverages ....Serving Size per Person
Champagne ....2 4-ounce glasses
Coffee (regular or instant) ....1½ cups
Tea ....1½ cups
Cocoa .... 1 cup
Dinner wine .... 4 ounces
Dessert wine .... 3 ounces

● Bread and Rolls

Bread .... 1-2 slices
Rolls .... 1½ -2 rolls

● Meat

Beef

Hamburger .... 2½ ounces
Roast (bone in or boneless) .... 3 ounces
Steak (boneless) .... 4 ounces
Steak (bone in) .... 5 ounces
Stew (vegetable recipe) ....3 ounces of meat

Lamb

Chops .... 2 chops
Roast (bone in or boneless) .... 3 ounces
Pork (fresh)
Chops .... 2 chops
Roast (bone in or boneless) .... 3 ounces
Sausage (patty or link) .... 3 ounces
Spareribs .... 6 ounces

Pork (cured)

Bacon .... 2 slices
Ham (uncooked bone in or boneless) .... 3 ounces
Ham (fully cooked boneless) .... 3 ounces

Miscellaneous

Cold cuts .... 2 ounces
Frankfurters .... 2 or 1½ ounces

Fish and Seafood

Shrimp (shelled) .... 3-4 ounces
Lobster or crab (in shell) .... 8 ounces
Fish steaks or fillets .... 5 ounces

● Poultry

Chicken

Broilers.. half
Fryers (cut up)..8 ounces
Fish steaks or fillets ....5 ounces
Whole (roasted and meat striped from bones).....................4 ounces

Vegetables

Frozen..½ cup
Canned..½ cup
Potatoes (baked)..1 medium
Potatoes (creamed, mashed, scalloped)...........................½ cup
Lettuce (mixed green salad)..............................6 per head
Tomatoes (sliced)..4 slices
Carrots, celery (sticks)..3 ounces
Radishes..2-3

Fruits

Fresh (sectioned and pared)....................................½ cup
Grapes (fresh bunches) ....½ cup
Melon (cantaloupe, etc.)... half
Melon (watermelon)....................................1 inch thick slice
Canned..½ cup

Desserts

Cake .... 1 piece or 3 inch square
Pie ....1 piece
Ice Cream or Sherbet...⅔ cup

Dairy Products

Milk..8 ounces
Butter... 1-1½ pats
Butter (for vegetables).......................................1 teaspoon
Cream for coffee .... 1 tablespoon
Eggs (scrambled)..½ cup

Condiments

Catsup, mustard, relish..............................½ -1 tablespoons
Jam, jelly .... 1½ -2 tablespoons
Olives 2-4
Pickles..1 medium
Mayonnaise..1½ tablespoons
Salad dressing (liquid)............................. 1 tablespoon

Prepared Foods

Potato or macaroni salad...½ cup
Baked beans.. 1 cup
Spaghetti (uncooked)...1½ cups
Spaghetti sauce..¼-½ cup
Gravy (for meats)..2 tablespoons
Dressing (bread or rice)..½ cup
Rice..½ cup

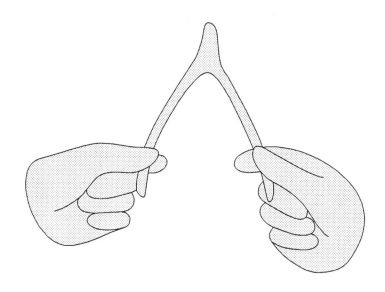

If you boil vegetables and find an objectionable odor associated with them, add 1-2 tablespoons of vinegar to the water.

Wines For Cooking

Foods ....Amount............Type of Wine

Sauces

Brown Sauce ....1 tablespoon per cup ....Sherry or Burgundy

Cheese Sauce ....1 tablespoon per cup ....Sherry or Sauterne

Cream Sauce ....1 tablespoon per cup ....Sherry or Sauterne

Dessert Sauce ....1 tablespoon per cup ....Port or Muscatel

Tomato Sauce ....1 tablespoon per cup ....Sherry or Burgundy

Meats

Gravy for Roasts ....1 tablespoon per cup ....Burgundy, Sauterne, Sherry

Ham.....................................2 cups (basting) ....Port or Muscatel

Lamb.......................3 tablespoons per pound (basting) ....Sauterne, Dry Vermouth

Roasts ....3 tablespoons per pound (basting) ....Burgundy

Steaks & Chops.........3 tablespoons per pound (basting) ....Burgundy

Poultry and Game Meats

Chicken.....................3 tablespoons per pound (basting) ....Sauterne, Burgundy, Dry Vermouth

Duck ....3 tablespoons per pound (basting) ....Burgundy

Gravy for Chicken ....1 tablespoon per cup ....Sauterne, Burgundy, Sherry

Pheasant ....3 tablespoons per pound (basting) ....Sauterne, Burgundy, Sherry

Turkey ....¼ cup per 5/lbs (basting) ....Sauterne or Dry Vermouth

Venison.....................3 tablespoons per pound (basting) ....Burgundy

Fish

Whole, fillets or steaks ....½ cup per lb. (basting) ....Sauterne, Dry Vermouth

Things Learned the Hard Way

● Murphy's Law applies to cooking:

1. Anything that can go wrong, will.

2. Left to themselves, things always go from bad to worse.

3. If there is a possibility of several things going wrong, the one that will go wrong is the one that will do the most damage.

4. If everything seems to be going well, you have obviously overlooked something.

5. Ingredients are always expressed in the least usable terms. Quantity, for example, will be expressed in dessertspoons per scant liters.

6. If a recipe requires "X" ingredients, there will be "X-1" ingredients in stock.

7. A dropped kitchen utensil will land where it can do the most damage. (Also known as the law of selective gravitation.)

● Set a timer when something is to come out of the oven or should be "turned down" after a certain number of minutes.

● A whole lemon will keep perfectly and almost indefinitely if submerged in a jar of water kept in the refrigerator. To get more juice, drop it briefly in boiling water. Use only the yellow oily skin for grated lemon rind, that's where the flavor is. The next layer down is just bitter.

● Never cook a steak too long or too fast. Always serve it sizzling hot. Pork and poultry should be cooked well done.

● Use mixes if you know they are good. "Near East" brand rice pilaf is better than if made from scratch.

● Don't salt with a heavy hand. Guests can add more if they wish. If your soup or stew is too salty, add some cut up raw potatoes. Scoop them out and throw away once they have cooked and absorbed some of the salt. You might also try adding 1 teaspoon of cider vinegar and 1 teaspoon sugar.

● Herbs should be subtle, not overpowering. Taste as you cook. Some flavors get stronger as they cook while others tend to cook away.

- A soufflé doesn't like to wait for a late guest. It must be served immediately or it will fall.

- Enjoy your party, but don't try to do too much. Plan ahead so everything will be done at once. For example, potatoes will bake in the oven along with your roast, but if the oven is set at 325° or 350°, allow at least a half hour longer than when baking 1 hour at 450°. Don't program the roast to match the potatoes, or you'll end up with a burnt offering. Jot down the menu to be prepared and note the time each item requires attention. Also, this reminds you of something you might have stashed in the refrigerator and sometimes forget to serve.

- Rice expands when cooked. Likewise a few other groceries:

  1 cup dry rice = $3\frac{1}{2}$ cups cooked

  1 cup macaroni or pasta = 2 cups cooked

  $\frac{1}{2}$ pound cheese = 2 cups grated

  1 cup whipping cream = slightly over 2 cups whipped

  1 cup beans = $2\frac{1}{2}$ cups cooked

- Wash dishes before the kitchen becomes utter chaos. Save some dish washing by keeping a measuring cup in the sugar and flour canisters, a teaspoon in the baking power and a tablespoon in the coffee can.

- Set out all ingredients before starting to mix. Put everything to the right of the bowl and after measuring out what you need, place the container to the left. Then, when you are interrupted or start daydreaming, you know how far you've progressed and don't omit something and add another twice. (My little sister once made sugar cookies and forgot the sugar).

- When beating egg whites, use a clean bowl and beater. A speck of grease will prevent beating to a good volume. Even a speck of egg yolk is detrimental. Should the yolk break, use the egg shell to capture it. A spoon just won't do it.

- Do everything you can before guests arrive. If you are making individual omelettes or any dish that must be done at the last minute, enlist a guest to break and beat eggs while you preside over the range.

- Don't be squeamish about getting your hands in the food. Pie crust and dough can't be made any other way. If a spoon or fork doesn't work, get right in there.

Food and Cooking Hints

BROWN SUGAR

If your brown sugar turns hard as a rock, place the open package on a pan next to a cup of water. Place in an oven at low heat for several minutes until the sugar is soft.

EGGS

When shopping for or using eggs, the color of the shell or yolk has nothing to do with the quality of the egg or its nutritious value. Our chickens lay colored and spotted eggs. And, we even use duck eggs (mostly for baking since they are sweeter than chicken eggs). When storing the eggs, place them small end down in the refrigerator. To check for freshness, place the egg in the bottom of a pan of cold water. If it lies on its side, it is fresh. If it stands at an angle, it is at least three days old and ten days old if it stands on end. If it rises to the surface, throw it out. If you forget whether your eggs are raw or hard-boiled, spin them. Hard-boiled eggs spin round and round, raw eggs wobble instead of spinning. Extra large eggs are good for eating; medium to large eggs are best for baking. (See Hard Boiled Eggs)

FAT

If there is too much fat on your creation, place it in the refrigerator until the fat coagulates and hardens on the top, then scrape off with a spoon. When cooking soups or stews, remove the fat by placing some ice cubes in the pot and stir. Scoop the ice cubes out before they melt and the fat clings to them.

FISH

If you purchase frozen fish, do so in a quantity than can be totally used once it is thawed out. Never refreeze after thawing.

FRYING PAN

Before using a new frying pan, boil vinegar to prevent foods from sticking. Before frying or sautéing foods, heat the pan before adding butter or oil to prevent sticking. If the food has a tendency to spatter, add a little salt.

GRAVY

Brown the flour well before adding the liquid portion to help eliminate lumps. Be sure to mix the flour and/or cornstarch into a smooth paste before adding it gradually. Then stir constantly while bringing it to a boil. If the gravy is greasy, add a small amount of baking soda.

HARD BOILED EGGS

Place eggs in pan with cold water and 2 tablespoons vinegar and 1 teaspoon salt. If the eggs crack while cooking, the vinegar will keep the white from running out of the shells. Bring to a boil, reduce heat and simmer 5- to 8-minutes. Rinse in cold water, then shake the pan back and forth to crack the shells. Peel.

HONEY

To measure honey (or other sticky syrups), use cooking oil to coat the spoon or cup and rinse it in hot water.

STEAKS

Club Steak — One of the smaller loin steaks. Excellent for barbecuing. Allow one steak, 1 inch thick, per person.

Rib Steak — This is one of the tastiest beef cuts. Each steak is cut from the entire rib section. Allow one steak per person.

Round Steak — This and similar cuts should be marinated and tenderized. It needs to cook longer than other steaks. Allow ¾ pound per serving.

Sirloin Steak — The largest of the loin steaks. This cut is great for serving a crowd of people. Allow ¾ pound per person.

T-Bone Steak — This is similar in size to the club steak and easily recognized by the shape of the bone. Allow about 1 pound per person.

Tenderloin Steak — This is known as the tenderloin or filet mignon. It comes from the smaller muscle of a porterhouse steak. It is the very best. Allow ½ pound per serving.

ROASTS

Beef Brisket — Cook long and slow in a double sheet of foil on the grill. Allow ¾ pound per person.

Bone Chuck Roast — Marinate and use a meat tenderizer if this is not a prime grade of meat. Cook right on the grill, turning and basting from time to time. Allow 1 pound per person.

Rib Eye Roast — This is the choice, tender eye muscle of the rib. There is no bone. Allow ½ pound per person.

Sirloin Tip Roast — An economical and tasty roast for spit cooking. There is no bone. Allow ½ pound per person.

Standing Rib Roast — This is the favorite for cooking on a spit. Be sure to tie and fasten firmly. Allow about 1 pound per person.

MILK

Be careful to always keep the cap or cover of milk containers tightly closed. Milk has a propensity for absorbing odors from other foods.

ONIONS

Refrigerate before chopping to reduce your tears. Try cutting the root end off the onion first and peel it in cold running water. Use fresh lemon juice to wash hands and remove the onion scent.

POULTRY

Never refreeze poultry after thawing. When defrosting, place it in a water proof plastic bag or cover with plastic wrap before soaking in water or the flavor will be dissipated. After handling chicken, wash your hands thoroughly before touching any other food items. A good way to cause food poisoning (botulism) is to handle chicken and then make a salad.

SALT SHAKER

Add some rice grains (5 or 10) to the inside of your shaker to keep the top from clogging.

STOCK POT

When cooking rice, spaghetti or noodles, add a small lump of butter or a few teaspoons of cooking oil to the water to keep the mixture from boiling over or sticking together.

VEGETABLES

Store potatoes in a cool, dark place. Keep your onions separate from other foods that could absorb their odor.

☞ Use 1 heaping tablespoonful of coffee for each 2 cups to be brewed.

Equivalents

IF YOU DON'T HAVE ....SUBSTITUTE

Active dry yeast, 1 package.................. 1 cake compressed yeast

Buttermilk, 1 cup .... 1 cup whole milk +
.... 1 tbsp. lemon juice or vinegar

Chocolate, 1 oz. unsweetened.. 3 tablespoons unsweetened cocoa
..................................powder + 1 tablespoon butter

Cornstarch, 1 tablespoon for thickening .... 2 tablespoons
....all-purpose flour

Dry mustard, 1 teaspoon.............. 1 tablespoon prepared mustard

Flour, 1 cup cake.......... 1 cup less 2 tablespoons all-purpose flour

Garlic, 1 clove.....................................⅛ teaspoon garlic powder
.... or minced dried garlic

Lemon peel, 1 teaspoon finely shredded .... ½ teaspoon
.... lemon extract

Milk, 1 cup whole ....½ cup evaporated milk + ½ cup water

Mustard, 1 teaspoon dry .... 1 tablespoon prepared mustard

Onion, 1 small .... 1 teaspoon onion
..............................powder or 1 tablespoon minced dried onion

Sugar, 1 cup granulated .... 2 cups sifted powdered sugar

Sugar, 1 cup granulated .... 1 cup packed brown sugar

Tomato sauce, 2 cups ....¾ cup tomato paste + 1 cup water

Tomato juice, 1 cup ....½ cup tomato sauce + ½ cup water

Notes:

Food Conversions

FOOD..............AMOUNT BEFORE...........AMOUNT AFTER

FOOD	AMOUNT BEFORE	AMOUNT AFTER
Almond nuts	1 pound in shell	¼ cup shelled
Apples	1 medium	1 cup sliced
Apricots	1 pound (3 cups)	4¾ cups cooked
Baking powder	1 cup	5½ ounces
Bananas	1 medium	⅛ cup mashed
Beans, Navy	1 pound (2 cups)	6 cups cooked
Beans, dried kidney	1 pound (2 ⅔ cups)	6½ cups cooked
Beans, dried lima	1 pound (3 cups)	7 cups cooked
Beans, dried	1 pound (2½ cups)	6 cups cooked
Boneless meat	1 pound raw	2 cups cooked
Butter	1 pound	2 cups
Cabbage	1 pound (1 small)	5 cups shredded
Carrots	1 pound (6 to 8 medium)	3 cups shredded
Carrots	1 pound (6 to 8 medium)	2½ cups chopped
Celery	1 medium bunch	4½ cups chopped
Cereal, oats (quick)	1 pound (4 cups)	8 cups cooked
Cereal, rolled oats	8 ounces (5½ cups)	2¾ quarts cooked
Cheese	1 pound	2 ⅔ cups cubed
Cheese	4 ounces	1 cup shredded
Cocoa	1 pound	4 cups ground
Cooked meat	1 pound	3 cups chopped
Cornmeal	1 pound	3 cups
Cornstarch	1 pound	3 cups
Eggs	1 egg	4 tablespoons liquid
Eggs	4 to 5 whole	1 cup
Eggs	7 to 9 whites	1 cup
Eggs	12 to 14 yolks	1 cup
Flour	1 pound cake	4½ cups
Flour	1 pound all-purpose	4 cups
Graham crackers	14 squares	1 cup finely crushed
Green peppers	1 large	1 cup chopped
Lemons	1 medium	3 tablespoons juice

(FOOD CONVERSIONS - continued)

FOOD	AMOUNT BEFORE	AMOUNT AFTER
Lemons	1 lemon rind	1 tablespoon grated
Lemons	5 to 8 medium	1 cup
Long grain rice	1 cup (7 ounces)	3 cups cooked
Macaroni	1 cup (3½ ounces)	2½ cups cooked
Mushrooms	1 pound (6 cups)	2 cups cooked
Noodles	3 cups (4 ounces)	3 cups cooked
Nuts, peanuts	1 pound	2 cups meats
Nuts, pecans	1 pound	2¼ cups meats
Nuts, walnuts	1 pound	2 cups meats
Onions	1 medium	½ cup chopped
Oranges	1 medium	¼ cup juice
Oranges	1 rind	1 to 2 tablespoons grated
Pecans	1 pound in shell	2 cups shelled
Popcorn	¼ cup	5 cups cooked
Potatoes	1 medium	½ cup mashed
Quick-cooking rice	1 cup (3 ounces)	2 cups cooked
Raisins	1 pound (3 cups)	4 cups cooked
Shortening	1 pound	2 cups
Spaghetti	8 ounces	4 cups cooked
Sugar	1 pound granulated	2 cups
Sugar	1 pound brown	2½ cups
Sugar	1 pound powdered	3½ cups
Sugar	1 pound cubes	96 to 160 cubes
Tomatoes	1 medium	½ cup cooked
Walnuts	1 pound in shell	1½ cups shelled
Whipping cream	1 cup	2 cups whipped

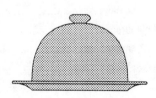

Procedures and Definitions

ACHIOTE (ANNATTO) - Occasionally you may run across this ingredient in a Mexican recipe book. If you can't find these brown-orange seedes at your local market, don't worry about it. They are for the most part tasteless. Their purpose in any recipe is to provide an orange color (used in cheddar cheese, butter and smoked fish). The seeds come from the tropical annatto tree.

APPETIZER - A small serving of food or beverage served before or as the first course of a meal.

ASPIC - Fish, meat or vegetable stock that has been thickened with gelatin to make a well-seasoned jelly.

AU GRATIN - A term usually applied to a scalloped dish (such as scalloped potatoes) meaning that it has a browned covering or crust of bread crumbs which have been mixed with butter and/or cheese.

BAKE - To cook in an oven with dry heat.

BARBECUE - To roast, broil or grill meat over live coals or an open flame, usually basting it with a highly seasoned sauce.

BASTE - To brush or ladle melted fat, drippings or sauces over food while cooking. It is usually done to meat while it is roasting in order to make it and keep it moist.

BATTER - A mixture of flour, liquid, salt or sugar, that is stirred or beaten.

BEAT - To mix vigorously with a brisk motion using an over and over or rapid rotary motion, making the mixture smooth, while adding air.

BISQUE - A rich thick cream soup usually made from fish. Also a rich frozen dessert, usually containing powdered or finely chopped nuts or macaroons.

BLANCH - To plunge the meat of nuts or fruit into boiling water for a couple of minutes, then in cold water. This loosens the skin for easier removal; to pour boiling water over a food, then drain and rinse with cold water. Used to whiten or to remove skins as from almonds.

BLEND - To combine two or more ingredients together thoroughly so that each loses its individual identity.

BOIL - To cook in a liquid which is kept above the boiling point, where the liquid is placed over high heat until bubbles rise rapidly and continuously.

BONBON - A sweet made of or dipped into fondant.

BOUILLABAISE - A chowder made of several varieties of fish and white wine.

BOUILLON - A clear, delicately seasoned soup made from lean meat stock, usually beef or chicken.

BRAISE - To brown meat by broiling, baking or frying, then to cover it and simmer until it is tender, keeping the temperature low and adding a small amount of liquid; to cook meat by searing in fat, then simmering in a covered dish in a small amount of moisture.

BREW - To steep or let stand in hot water to extract the essence of flavor, as in tea.

BROIL - To cook with direct heat. It is usually done by cooking between two heated surfaces; although, meat can be broiled over hot coals.

BRUSH - To spread thinly over food.

BUTTERFLY CUT - To hold a cut of meat vertically on its edge, slice down the center to within ½ the thickness of the meat (for example, a 1 inch thick steak is sliced down to within ½ inch of the cutting board), and fold the two parts flat to form a larger cut of meat.

CAFFEINE - An alkaloidal substance found in the coffee bean, coffee leaf, tea leaf, yerba mate, cacao bean. The content in a cup of coffee is about 1.5 grains; in tea less than 1 grain.

CANAPÉ - An appetizer made of a small piece of bread spread with a highly seasoned food.

CARAMEL or CARAMELIZE - To heat dry sugar over low heat to a liquid state until it becomes a golden brown. The pan is usually moved on and off the heat source to keep from burning.

CASSEROLE DISH - A dish made of glass, earthenware or cast iron in which food is baked and served.

CAVIAR - Salted roe (fish eggs). Originally from sturgeon.

CAPON - A castrated male chicken. Grows large and has tender meat.

CHAFING DISH - A dish set above a heat source, used to either cook or maintain the warmth of food at the table.

CHANTILLY - A dish in which whipped or plain cream is one of the ingredients.

CHARLOTTE or CHARLOTTE RUSSE - A gelatin dessert with flavored whipped cream molded in a form lined with cake.

CHICORY - The root of a plant that is cut into slices, dried and roasted as coffee. Leaves of the plant are used for salad and sometimes called curly endive.

CHOP - Cut into pieces of desired size.

CHOWDER - A dish made of fresh fish, or clams, pork, crackers and onions, which is stewed together.

CIDER - The juice pressed from apples used as a beverage or to make vinegar.

COBBLER - A deep-dish fruit pie with a rich biscuit dough used instead of pasty.

COCKTAIL - An appetizer served before or as the first course of a meal; an alcoholic beverage usually served before dinner; fruit or vegetable juice; cut fruit or shellfish with tart sauce served as first course.

CODDLE - Cook in water just below the boiling point.

COMBINE - To mix ingredients.

COMPOTE - Sweetened stewed fruit, cooked to keep the fruit as whole as possible.

CONDIMENTS - Food seasonings such as salt, vinegar, herbs and spices.

CONSOMMÉ - A highly seasoned clear soup made from one or a combination of meats.

CORN ON THE COB - Use a large stock pot with enough water to cover the corn (about ⅓ full). Place 1½ teaspoons of salt and 1 tablespoon butter in the water and bring it to a boil. Pull the husks from the ears of the corn. Place the corn in the boiling water. When water begins to boil again, reduce heat to gentle boil for about 7 minutes or until soft. When done the kernals can be easily penetrated with the tines of a fork.

CRACKLINGS - Crisp particles left after fat has been fired out.

CREAM - To manipulate with a spoon or a beater until soft and waxy; to work foods until soft and fluffy. Usually applied to shortening and sugar.

CREAM TOGETHER - Rinse a bowl with hot water and use a wooden spoon to press butter against the walls of the bowl until soft. Slowly add sugar while mixing continuously. An electric mixer is nice for this, but not a necessity.

CROQUETTES - Cooked food that has been chopped and is held together by a thick white sauce. Many times it is covered with crumbs and eggs and fried in deep fat; a mixture of chopped or ground cooked food held together by eggs on a thick sauce, shaped, dipped into egg and crumbs and fried.

CROUTONS - Bread cut into small cubes and toasted in an oven for use in salads and soups. These can be homemade or purchased.

CRUMB - To dip food into or roll in cracker or bread crumbs.

CUSTARD - A cooked or baked mixture mainly of eggs and milk. It may be sweetened to use as a dessert or flavored with cheese or fish, as an entrée.

CUT - To divide foods with a knife or scissors; to incorporate solid fat into dry ingredients with the least amount of blending, so the fat remains in small particles.

CUT IN SHORTENING - To mix shortening with flour by using a pastry blender or large fork or two knives used like scissors until the shortening is evenly distributed, usually in bean sized chunks. This does not mean that the shortening is totally dissolved or melted.

CUTLET - A small piece of meat cut from the leg or rib of veal or pork, or a croquette mixture made into the shape of a cutlet.

DASH - Less than ⅛ teaspoon of an ingredient.

DEEP FRY - (see FRY) - to cook in fat which completely covers the food.

DEVILED - Highly seasoned or spicy hot by adding condiments.

DICE - Cut into small cubes.

DOLLOP - A large lump, helping or portion, such as ice cream, whipping cream or sour cream.

DOUBLE BOILER - One pan nested within another in which water is added to the bottom pan up to the base of the inner pan. This allows slow, even cooking of food by the action of the boiling water in the bottom pan.

DREDGE - To coat well, usually with flour or sugar.

DRIPPINGS - The fat and juices which cook out of meat or poultry.

DUST - To sprinkle lightly, usually with flour or sugar.

ENTRÉE - The main dish of an informal meal or a subordinate dish served between main courses.

FLAKE - To break lightly into small pieces with a fork.

FLORENTINE - Dishes named "florentine" contain spinach, with the exception of "alla fiorentina" found on Italian menus. Here it means the dish has been prepared in the traditional manner of Florence.

FOLD or FOLD IN - Gently mix two or more ingredients together with down, across, up and over motion, causing the liquid from the bottom to be moved to the top. This creates a blend of the mixture without releasing air bubbles; usually applied to adding beaten egg whites or whipped cream to a mixture.

FONDANT - A sugar and water mixture cooked to the soft-ball stage (234°F.), cooled and kneaded.

FONDUE - A hot dish made by melting cheese and adding ingredients such as wine, eggs, butter, milk, bread crumbs, etc., and served with bread; a baked food similar to a soufflé but including bread or cracker crumbs.

FONDUE POT - A metal or ceramic pot that incorporates a stand to hold it above a heat source.

FRAPPÉ - Sweetened fruit juice frozen until of mushy consistency.

FRENCH FRY - (See FRY) - to cook in enough fat to completely cover the food.

FRICASSEE - Cook meat by stewing it in gravy.

FRITTERS - Fruit, meat, vegetables or fish covered with batter or chopped and mixed with batter. Usually fried in deep fat.

FRY - To cook in hot fat. To PAN FRY or SAUTÉ is to cook in a small amount of fat. To FRENCH FRY or DEEP FRY is to cook in enough fat deep enough to completely cover the food.

GARNISH - To ornament with something bright and savory. Something added for decoration.

GELATIN - A purified protein found in connective tissues and bones of animals.

GIBLETS - The heart, liver and gizzard of poultry.

GLACÉ - To coat with a thin sugar syrup that has been cooked to crack stage.

GOULASH - A thick meat stew originating in Hungary.

GRATE - To divide into small pieces by rubbing on a rough surface. A vegetable grate is a metal utensil with protruding holes used to cut off small pieces of vegetables or cheese.

GRILL - To cook with direct heat. It is usually done by cooking over hot coals.

HOLLANDAISE - A rich sauce made of eggs and butter, served hot with vegetables and fish.

HORS D'OEUVRES - Salty, tart or crisp foods served as appetizers, such as canapés, fish, pickles, olives, celery and sausages.

INDIENNE - A term encountered on some French menus indicating the dish contains contains curry.

INFUSION - Liquid extracted from coffee, tea or herbs.

JULIENNE - Cut into long thin strips; food such as cheese, meat, etc., that is sliced similar to match sticks.

KNEAD - To work dough with the hands, using a folding-back and pressing-forward motion. To squeeze, fold and stretch the dough into a consistent mixture.

LARD - To cover meat, fish or poultry with strips or slices of fat, or to insert strips of fat under the skin or into the flesh with a skewer.

LEAVEN - To cause baked foods to rise by adding a leavening agent.

MACEDOINE - A mixture of vegetables or fruits. The term comes from Alexander the Great. He lived in Macedonia, a country made up from many smaller states.

MARINARA SAUCE - An Italian term meaning "sailor style." This is a combination of tomatoes, red wine, anchoives and garlic.

MARINATE - To let food stand for some amount of time in a well-seasoned acid and oil mixture.

MARZIPAN - A paste of sweet almonds and sugar.

MASK - To completely cover with a thick sauce, jelly or mayonnaise.

MELT - To liquefy by heat.

MERINGUE - A mixture of stiffly beaten egg whites, flavoring and sugar. Used on pies and tarts.

MINCE - Chop very fine. Much finer than to dice.

MINESTRONE - A thick Italian vegetable soup.

MIX To combine in any manner that effects distribution.

MOCHA - A flavoring made with coffee infusion or with coffee infusion and chocolate.

MOLD - To shape food, usually by pouring the liquified food into a mold. When the liquid is cooled it will retain the shape of the mold.

MOUSSE - A mixture of whipped cream, sugar and flavoring frozen without stirring. Or flavored thin cream and gelatin combined with meat, fruits or vegetables.

MUFFIN - A drop batter baked in individual pans and served as a quick bread.

NOUVELLE CUISINE - Some young French chefs conspired to create a new way of cooking for the health-conscious public. They eliminated the heavy, rich sauces and created lighter dishes with fresh vegetables, fish and small portions.

PAN-BROIL - To cook in a hot frying pan with little or no fat or pouring off fat as it accumulates.

PAN-FRY - (see FRY) - to cook in a small amount of fat.

PARBOIL - To boil or simmer a raw food until partially cooked and tender as a preliminary to another method of cooking.

PARCH - To brown by means of dry heat. Applied to grains.

PARE - Cut off the outside covering of apples, potatoes and the like.

PARFAIT - A frozen dessert made of a foundation of beaten egg whites or yolks cooked with hot syrup, sometimes with whipped cream added. Also applied to ice cream and syrup served in parfait glasses.

PASTEURIZE - To preserve food by heating sufficiently to destroy micro-organisms and arrest fermentation. Applied to liquids such as milk and fruit juices.

PÂTÉ DE FOIE GRAS - Paste made from goose liver, often with truffles, spread on crackers or bread.

PEEL - Strip off the outer covering of fruits and vegetables such as oranges and grapefruit.

POACH - To cook in water kept just below the boiling point.

PURÉE - To press through a coarse sieve.

RAGOUT - A thick highly seasoned stew.

RELISH - A highly seasoned food used as an accompaniment.

RENDER - To free fat from connective tissue by heating until the fat melts and can be drained off.

ROAST - To cook in an oven by dry heat; uncovered and with no liquid added. Essentially the same as BAKE, but the term used for meats.

ROE - Eggs of fish.

ROLL - To place on a board and spread thin with a rolling pin.

SAUTÉ - To cook quickly in a frying pan by shifting and stirring the food constantly from side to side in a small quantity of oil.

SCALD - To bring a liquid, such as milk, to a temperature below the boiling point at which bubbles appear around the sides of the surface. Milk scorches easily and should be scalded in a double boiler, rather than over direct heat. If a double boiler is not available, control heat by moving the cooking vessel on and off the heat source.

SCALLOP - To bake food which has been divided into small pieces and mixed or arranged in layers with a sauce in a baking dish. Buttered crumbs are often sprinkled over the top. (see AU GRATIN)

SCORE - To cut narrow gashes along the surface.

SEAR - To cook at a very high temperature for a short time in order to quickly form a brown crust on the outer surface of meat.

SHERBET - Frozen mixture of fruit juice, sugar, egg whites and milk or water.

SHIRR - To break eggs into a dish with cream or crumbs and bake in an oven.

SHRED - To cut or tear in thin strips.

SIFT - To put dry ingredients through a fine sieve.

SIMMER - To cook in a liquid at a heat range less than boiling, but sufficient to form small, slowly rising bubbles where the liquid is practically motionless. The temperature is about 185°F. Most foods are simmered after reaching the boil stage. The heat is turned low and you see only lady-like bubbles.

SKEWER - A wood or metal pin used to hold foods together (such as attaching bacon around the outside edges of a steak) or to hold foods in shape while cooking.

SORBET - A sherbet made from a mixture of fruits similar to a frappé and having a mushy consistency. Often served before the first course of dinner to cleanse the palate.

SOUFFLÉ - A dish made very light and puffy by the addition of beaten egg whites.

STEAM - To cook by contact with live steam in a closed container, such as a perforated container placed over boiling water.

STEEP - To let stand in hot liquid below the boiling point for the purpose of extracting flavor or color or both.

STEW - To cook slowly in liquid held below the boiling point.

STIR - To blend ingredients, using a circular motion.

STOCK - The basis for making soup or gravy. It is made by extracting the soluble parts of meat, fish, poultry or vegetables.

THICKEN - Clear soup is very thin. When desirable to change the consistency or texture to a fuller body in order to change from a stimulating appetizer to a main course, the most common way of thickening is to use 1 to 2 teaspoons of flour mixed with 2 to 4 teaspoons of cold water (Place in a jar and shake to mix). This is formed into a paste which is *slowly* added to the boiling soup while stirring. Another method used to THICKEN is to add some "home made" noodles. These can be purchased in various widths. The noodles will expand, so don't use too many.

TOAST - To brown by direct heat or in a hot oven.

TRUFFLES - Sometimes called the élite of mushrooms. These are expensive, odoriferous, little potato-shaped fungi rooted out from beneath oak trees by trained pigs (sometimes dogs).

VEGETABLE MARROW - An egg shaped gourd about 8 to 10 inches long. A vegetable.

VICHYSSOISE - A smooth leek-and-potato soup which is served chilled. Don't let the French name fool you, it was created at the Ritz Hotel in New York City.

WHIP - To beat rapidly with an egg beater or electric mixer until the cream is thick and doubles in bulk. Don't continue whipping or the cream will turn to butter.

WILD RICE - This is a "got-you," since wild rice isn't a rice at all, but rather the seeds from a water grass.

Herbs and Spices

The skillful use of various herbs and spices is the secret to creating distinctive dishes. They are used in salads, sauces, meats and desserts. While spices from all over the world can be purchased at the grocery store, many of the herbs can be home grown.

Spices wear out from being exposed to the air or after being stored for a long time. Be sure to keep them tightly covered.

ALLSPICE - This comes from the dried pea-sized berry of the pimento tree found in the Mexico, Jamaica, Central and South America and the West Indies. Its name arises from the fact that its flavor resembles a combination of cinnamon, cloves and nutmeg.

> Ground - It is used for cakes, puddings, relishes, and fruit preserves and baking.

> Whole - It is used for simmering meats and fish, pickles and gravies.

ANISE - This fruit from a small plant dries into a seed form coming mainly from Spain, Mexico and India. It has a licorice flavor and is used in coffee cakes, sweet rolls, cookies, breads and bread sticks.

BALM - This is a garden herb with a sharp lemon scent. It is used either fresh or dried in soups and salads.

BASIL - A plant grown in the United States and North Mediterranean areas, in which the leaves are dried, ground and powdered. It has an aromatic, leafy flavor. It is used in rich soups, stews, sauces, poultry, sausages and in tomato dishes.

BAY LEAVES - This is the aromatic leaf of the sweet-bay or laurel tree grown in the eastern Mediterranean countries. It is dried whole and used to flavor stews, spiced vinegars, soups, boiled fish, fish chowder, pot roasts and any tomato mixture.

BENE (SESAME) - Seed used on rolls, breads and buns.

CAPERS - The flower buds of Capparis spinosa grown in Mediterranean countries. Pickled and used as a condiment.

CARAWAY SEED - A herb from an aromatic fruit plant grown in the Netherlands. It is used in rye bread, cookies, cakes, candies, salads, cheese, sauerkraut, pork, liver, kidneys and canape spreads.

CARDAMOM SEED - This is obtained as a pod in which whole seeds are contained inside or as ground seeds. It is used in danish pastry, bun breads, coffee cakes, sliced oranges, grape jelly and cookies.

CASSIA - The bark from a tropical Asia tree similar to cinnamon but of inferior quality.

Ground: Used in baked goods.

Whole: It is used in pickling, preserving, puddings and stewed fruit.

CAYENNE or CAYENNE PEPPER - Sometimes called "red pepper," this is grown mainly in Africa. As a powder, it yields a hot, savory flavor used in meats, fish, sauces, egg dishes and cheese dishes.

CELERY SALT - This is a mixture of ground celery seed and fine white salt. It is used for meats, fish, boiled or fried eggs, potato salad, salad dressings, tomato juices and bouillon.

CELERY SEED - The seed of a small plant which has a similar appearance and taste to celery. It is used whole or ground for fish, potato salad, tomato dishes, pickling, salad dressings, stews and hamburgers.

CHERVIL - An apiaceous (umbelliferous) umbrella-like plant with aromatic leaves used to flavor soups and salads.

CHILI - A hot pepper used as a base for chili sauces and other spicy dishes.

CHILI POWDER - A mixture of ground red peppers (cayenne), cumin seed and other spices used to flavor chili con carne, other Mexican dishes, shellfish, cocktail sauces, boiled and scrambled eggs, gravy and stew seasoning, sea food cocktails and canned corn.

CHIVES - Similar to green onions although smaller in size and milder in taste.

CHUTNEY - A spicy pickle of compound fruit and seasonings.

CINNAMON - True cinnamon grows only in Ceylon and is the product of the inner bark of Cinnamon zeylancium. It is mild.

CASSIA CINNAMON - This is used more extensively than true cinnamon and has a greater full-bodied flavor. The bark is dried and then sold as sticks or ground. It is used in pickling, preserving, baked products and for beverages.

CLOVES - The flower buds of a tree which is used whole or ground.

Whole - Roast pork or ham, pickling fruits, spiced sweet syrups.

CLOVES - (continued)

Ground - Baked goods, puddings, potato soup, borscht and stews.

CORIANDER - An herb, *Coriandrum sativum*, with aromatic seeds used whole or ground.

Whole - Mixed pickles, apple pie, pea soup, gingerbread, cookies, cakes, biscuits, poultry stuffing, mixed green salads and confections.

Ground - In sausages, fresh pork, other meats and on buns.

CUMIN or CUMINSEED - This has a slightly bitter flavor. The SEED flavors liqueurs, cheeses, bread, meats, sausages and pickles. POWDERED it is used in curry powder.

CURRY POWDER - A yellow condiment from India containing a blend of ginger, turmeric, fenugreek seed, and as many as 16 to 20 spices used for curry sauce, meat, fish, eggs, chicken, cream soup, tomato soup, French dressing and fish chowder.

DILL or DILL SEED - The seed of an herb grown in India, having a clean, aromatic taste used in pickles, sauces, sauerkraut, salads, soups, fish and meat sauces, spiced vinegars and gravies.

DURKEE RED HOT - A commercially prepared hot sauce made from cayenne red peppers, vinegar, salt and garlic. Used for spaghetti, burgers, stews, chili, ribs, seafood, chicken, and soups. Excellent for buffalo-style chicken wings.

FENNEL - An herb producing seeds which are ground and used for boiled fish, pastries, apple pie, sweet pickles and candies. It resembles celery in looks and anise in flavor.

FINE HERBS - Chop separately ½ onion, 2 scallions, 2 springs of parsley, 1 tablespoon of leaf marjoram and ½ small leek and then combine to use in stews, soups, meat and fish stuffing, omelets, grilled meat, broth and for garnishing.

GARLIC - A plant of the lily family, the cloves of which produce a strong flavor for meats, salads and sauces.

GARLIC SALT - A mixture of garlic and fine white salt.

GINGER - As a root it is used in pickling, stewed dried fruits and applesauce.

Ground - it is used in cakes, pies, cookies, canned fruits and puddings.

HOT SAUCE - A commercially prepared hot sauce made from cayenne red peppers, vinegar, salt and garlic. Used for spaghetti, burgers, stews, chili, ribs, seafood, chicken and soups. Excellent for buffalo-style chicken wings.

LEEKS - A plant similar to an onion which has a strong flavor.

MACE - The blades around the nutmeg kernel. It is red when fresh and orange when dried.

Blades - are used in pickling, fish sauces, jellies and gingerbread.

Ground - it is used in yellow cakes, pound cakes, chocolate dishes and oyster stew.

MARJORAM - A plant from the mint family. The leaves are used whole or powdered.

Leaf - is used for stews, soups, sausages, poultry seasonings and lamb.

Powdered - it is used in soups, salads and stuffing.

MINCEMEAT SPICE - A mixture of spices such as cloves, allspice and cinnamon, used to flavor mincemeat, cakes, cookies and sauces.

MINT - A leaf plant used to flavor soups, vegetables, fruits and beverages. It may be used fresh or dried.

MSG (MONOSODIUM GLUTAMATE) - is a vegetable protein derivative for raising the effectiveness of natural food flavors. Used in small amounts (to taste) in steaks, roasts, chops, seafood, stews, soups, chowder, chop suey and cooked vegetables.

MUSTARD, DRY - Whole or ground seeds used in pickles, meats, sauces, gravies and salads. When combined with vinegar and spices it is known as *prepared mustard.*

NUTMEG - The fruit of the Myristica tree produces four parts: an outer husk, the mace, an inner shell, and the nutmeg seed. NUTMEG comes whole or ground and is used in baked goods, sauces, puddings and vegetables.

OLD BAY SEASONING - A product of the Baltimore Spice Company, Baltimore, Maryland 21208, used for seafood, poultry, salads and meats. It contains a mixture of celery salt, pepper, mustard, pimento, cloves, laurel leaves, mace, cardamom, ginger, cassia, paprika and monosodium glutamate.

ONION - A plant of the lily family which produces a strong distinctive flavor for meats, salads, soups and stews.

ONION SALT - A mixture of ground onion and fine white salt used to flavor meats, soups, salads and sauces.

OREGANO - Used in chili powder, for chili con carne and pork dishes.

PAPRIKA - A sweet red pepper (and excellent source of vitamin C) used for shellfish, fish, salad dressings and garnish.

PARSLEY - An herb used fresh or dried to flavor meats, vegetables, salads and soups. It makes an excellent garnish.

PEPPER (BLACK and WHITE) - Made from peppercorns which are the dried berries of a vine, Piper Nigrum.

Black pepper—made from the whole berry.

White pepper—made from what is left of the fully ripened berry after the outer coat has been removed. Used for pickling, soups and meats.

PIMENTO - The fleshy fruit of the Spanish paprika. Canned and used in meats, vegetable dishes and salads.

POPPY SEED - Used in breads, cakes, cookies and rolls.

POULTRY SEASONING - A prepared mixture of herbs and spices such as marjoram, sage and thyme, used for poultry, meat and fish stuffing.

PUMPKIN PIE SPICE - A mixture of spices such as cinnamon, cloves and ginger, used to flavor pumpkin pie.

ROSEMARY - Used to flavor and/or garnish fish, sauces and stews.

RED HOT - A commercially prepared hot sauce made from cayenne red peppers, vinegar, salt and garlic. Used for spaghetti, burgers, stews, chili, ribs, seafood, chicken and soups. Excellent for buffalo-style chicken wings.

SAFFRON - The stigma of a flower similar to a crocus, Crocus sativus. Dried and used to flavor meats and some breads. It has a rich orange-yellow color.

SAGE - A mint used in meat stuffing, head cheese, pork products and sausage.

SAUSAGE SEASONING - A mixture of spices such as white pepper, coriander and nutmeg.

SAVORY - A mint used fresh or dried.

SUMMER SAVORY - Leaves and flowers are used in salads, poultry and other stuffing, string beans, lima and broad beans.

WINTER SAVORY - Leaves and shoots (fresh or dried) used in sauces, stuffing and stews.

SCALLIONS - Small onions.

SESAME (BENE) - An herb producing seeds used on rolls, breads and buns.

SOY SAUCE - A very salty sauce commercially prepared from fermented soybeans.

TABASCO SAUCE - A highly seasoned hot sauce made from cayenne peppers, salt and vinegar.

TARRAGON - A perennial herb, the fresh or dried leaves of which are used in salads, pickles and vinegar.

THYME - An herb whose dried leaves are used to season soups, sauces, stuffing, cheese, meats, poultry and clams.

Cheese

AMERICAN

BRICK—Rennet cheese, with strong sweetish flavor, an elastic texture and many small round eyes or holes.

CHEDDAR—Similar to English-made Cheddar.

COTTAGE—Soft curds. Made commercially from pasteurized sour milk with or without rennet. Also known as *smierkase*.

CREAM—A soft rich cheese with mild flavor. Genuine cream cheese is made from pasteurized rich cream thickened by souring or from sweet cream thickened with rennet. It is also made from thin cream thickened with rennet and from whole milk.

HAND—Soft; sharp pungent taste and odor. Made from sour milk and shaped by hand. Caraway seeds are sometimes added.

HERKIMER—Aged Cheddar.

LIEDERKRANZ—Highly flavored soft cheese; milder than Limburger. Made in Ohio from milk set with rennet. Turns tawny yellow as it ripens.

PINEAPPLE—Hard, highly colored Cheddar made in pineapple shape, then hung and dried in a net, making diamond-shaped corrugations on the surface.

PROCESSED CHEESE—Cheese is blended with an emulsifying agent and pasteurized.

SAGE—A Cheddar cheese formerly made by adding sage leaves to the curd. Now a sage extract is usually used.

SWISS—Similar to Swiss-made Emmenthaler.

FOREIGN TYPES—Most of the cheeses formerly imported from Europe are now successfully produced in America.

ENGLISH-MADE

CHEDDAR—Hard, sharp, white or yellow color. Made from sweet milk and sold as *full cream* when whole milk is used, *part skim* or *skim*, depending on the type of milk used.

CHESHIRE—Hard rennet cheese somewhat like Cheddar.

STILTON—Hard rennet cheese with green or blue mold and wrinkled or ridged skin or rind.

FRENCH-MADE

BRIE—Soft, rennet cheese, definite odor, sharp flavor with a red color on the surface. Made from whole or partly skimmed milk.

CAMEMBERT—Soft, rennet cheese covered with a firm rind of molds and dried cheese.

COULOMMIERS—Soft rennet cheese, somewhat like Brie.

LIVEROT—Soft rennet cheese, somewhat like Brie. Made from partially skimmed milk. Has a strong piquant flavor.

NEUFCHÂTEL—Very soft rennet cheese, made from whole or skimmed milk.

PONT L'ÉVÊQUE—Soft rennet cheese, somewhat like Brie.

ROQUEFORT—Semihard rennet cheese with blue and green mold.

GERMAN-MADE

LIMBURGER—Soft rennet cheese with strong, characteristic odor.

MÜNSTER—Semihard rennet cheese, caraway seeds or aniseseeds added. Made from whole milk.

HOLLAND-MADE

EDAM—Hard rennet cheese, round with a red rind.

GOUDA—Hard rennet cheese, slightly round and flat.

LEYDEN—Hard rennet cheese. Cuminseed and cloves are added to the middle of 3 layers.

ITALIAN-MADE

CACIOCAVALLO—A hard, beet-shaped rennet cheese.

GORGONZOLA—Semihard rennet cheese with streaks of mold.

PARMESAN—Hard, rennet cheese made from partly skimmed milk. Green or black rind.

PROVOLI or PROVOLONI—Made from cows' or buffaloes' milk. Hard, round, smoked and held by a net.

REGGIANO—The best variety of Parmesan cheese.

SCANDINAVIAN-MADE

APPETITOST—Semihard, made from sour buttermilk.

GAMMELOST—Hard, made from skimmed sour milk, definite odor.

GJEDOST----Hard, made from goats' milk, chocolate-colored, sweet taste.

MYSOST----Semisoft whey cheese of mild sweetish flavor.

NOKKELOST----Hard, made from skimmed milk with spices.

SWISS-MADE

EMMENTHALER----Hard rennet cheese with large holes and a mild, somewhat sweetish flavor.

GRUYÈRE----Hard-blended rennet cheese with nut-like flavor.

SAP SAGO----Small, hard and green in color. It is used grated.

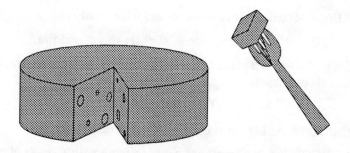

To remove onion or fish smell from your hands, wash with vinegar and water or salt and water or lemon juice and water.

Fats and Oils

BUTTER—Fat from sour or ripened cream gathered in a mass, sometimes salted and colored. It contains not less that 80% by weight of milk fat.

COMPOUND—A mixture of animal fats, a mixture of vegetable fats or a mixture of both.

CORN OIL—Refined oil from the dried, crushed corn germ.

COTTONSEED OIL—Refined oil from the crushed seed of the cotton plant.

CRACKLINGS—The residue from rendered fat of meat or poultry.

CREAM—The fat of milk that rises to the top when it stands.

DRIPPINGS—The fat obtained from cooking meats.

HYDROGENATED FATS—Oils or soft fats changed to solid fat by treatment with hydrogen.

LARD—Fat rendered from the fatty tissues of the hog.

NUT MARGARINE—Made from nut oils; coconut, peanut or palm oil.

OLEOMARGARINE—Made by churning a mixture of oils, milk and salt to a consistency similar to butter. It is used as a substitute for butter.

OLIVE OIL—Oil from the flesh of ripe olives. Virgin olive oil is that which is first extracted and is better in flavor and appearance than the oil produced by the second or third pressing.

PEANUT OIL—The oil extracted from peanuts. A by-product of peanut butter.

SUET—Clear, white fat of beef and mutton, usually from around the heart or kidney.

SWEET BUTTER—Made from sweet cream. Unsalted.

WHIPPED BUTTER—Butter into which air has been whipped.

Flour

ALL-PURPOSE FLOUR—A blend of hard or soft wheat flours, which is lower in protein than bread flour but higher than cake flour. It can be used with good results for all type of home baked products.

BRAN—A by-product of whole wheat flour. It contains some of the outer husk and some of the endosperm.

BREAD FLOUR—Milled from the inner part of hard or spring wheat.

BUCKWHEAT FLOUR—Milled from the finely ground buckwheat kernel.

CAKE FLOUR—Milled from soft wheat, the most highly refined flour milled; granulation uniform; protein content very low and also very delicate in quality.

CORN MEAL—Milled from corn.

WHOLE-WHEAT FLOUR—Milled from cleaned whole-wheat grain.

PASTRY FLOUR—Usually made of soft wheat; low in protein and finely milled, though not as fine as cake flour.

RICE FLOUR—Milled from rice.

RYE FLOUR—Milled from rye grain. More like wheat flour in bread making qualities than any other grain.

SELF-RISING FLOUR—Milled from soft or winter wheat and has salt and leavening added.

SOYBEAN FLOUR—Milled from the soybean.

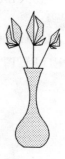

Weights and Measures

● **All measurements are level.**

1 dash	less than ⅛ teaspoon
60 drops	1 teaspoon (tsp.)
3 teaspoons (tsp.)	1 tablespoon (tbs. or tbsp.)
1 tablespoon (tbsp.)	½ fluid ounce (oz.)
2 tablespoons (tbsp.)	1 liquid ounce (oz.)
8 liquid ounces (oz.)	1 cup (c.)
4 tablespoons (tbsp.)	¼ cup (c.)
5 ⅓ tablespoons (tbsp.)	⅛ cup (c.)
8 tablespoons (tbsp.)	½ cup (c.)
10 ⅔ tablespoons (tbsp.)	⅔ cup (c.)
12 tablespoons (tbsp.)	¾ cup (c.)
16 tablespoons (tbsp.)	1 cup (c.)
½ cup (c.)	1 gill
1 cup (c.)	8 fluid ounces (oz.)
1 cup (c.)	½ pint (pt)
2 cups (c.)	1 pint (pt.)
2 pints (pt.)	1 quart (qt.)
4 quarts (qt.)	1 gallon (gal.)
4 cups (c.)	1 quart (qt.)
8 quarts (qt.)	1 peck
2 gallons (gal.)	1 peck
4 pecks	1 bushel (bu.)
16 ounces (oz.)	1 pound (lb.)
32 ounces (oz.)	1 quart (qt.)
1 ounce (oz.)	28.35 grams
1 pound (lb.)	453.59 grams
1 gram	0.035 ounces (oz.)
1 kilogram	2.2 pounds (lb.)
1 tablespoon	14.79 milliliters
1 cup (c.)	236.6 milliliters
1 quart	946.4 milliliters
1 liter	1.06 quarts
3 ounces	1 kilogram

Conversions/Equivalents

English..American

1 saltspoonful	¾ teaspoon (tsp.)
1 teaspoonful	1½ teaspoons
1 dessertspoonful	1 tablespoon (tbs. or tbsp.)
1 tablespoonful	2 tablespoons
1 teacupful	½ cup plus 2 tablespoons
1 breakfastcupful	1¼ cups
¼ pint (1 gill)	½ cup plus 2 tablespoons
½ pint (2 gills)	1¼ cups
1 pint	2½ cups
2 pints (1 quart)	5 cups

American Measures...................................Metric

1 teaspoon (tsp.)	approximately 5 cubic centimeters
1 tablespoon (tbs. or tbsp.)	approximately 15 cubic centimeters
1 cup	8 fluid ounces (236.6 cubic centimeters)
1 pint	16 fluid ounces
1 quart	32 fluid ounces
35 fluid ounces	1 liter

American Weights...............Metric Equivalents

½ ounce	15 grams
1 ounce	30 grams
1¾ ounces	50 grams
2½ ounces	75 grams
3½ ounces	100 grams
8½ ounces	255 grams
1 pound	505 grams
1 pound, 1½ ounces	550 grams
2 pounds, 3 ounces	1 kilogram

Index

Index

Index

Index

Index

Index

Order Form

Satisfaction guaranteed or return any books for a full refund.

This book demonstrates mountain flying can be fun and safe if good judgment and proper technique are exercised. It provides the prospective mountain pilot with the knowledge required for safe mountain flight. The experienced pilot will learn some new techniques and rules of thumb. Emphasizes all the hazards, dangers and special conditions inherent in mountain flight. The book is arranged in the sequence of a typical mountain flight.

Please send
_____ copies of:

Mountain Flying

Enclosed is $7.95 plus $1.75 shipping (75 cents for each additional book).

 Aurora Publications
7440 White Ash Place
Parker, Colorado 80134-5464
Telelphone (303) 841-8766

Name: _____

Company: _____

Address: _____

City: _____ State: _____ Zip: _____

PAYMENT: ☒ Check   Ⓒ VISA   Ⓒ MasterCard

Card # _____ Exp. Date: ___ / ___

Name on Card (if different from above) _____

Order Form

Satisfaction guaranteed or return any books for a full refund.

In this 82 minute video, which includes much in-fl action, you are taken through some of the most beauti rugged and demanding mountain terrain in the U There are segments on flight planning, accident cause weather, density altitutde, approachs, landings, depai tures and survival. The weather section includes time lapse sequences of thunderstorms, mountain waves, lenticular and rotor clouds. Graphics are used to clarify and explain the facts presented. It is useful to pilots of all skill levels and enhances safety in all types of flying, not just the mountains.

Please send
_____ copies of:

Enclosed is $49.95 plus $2.50 shipping (75 cents for each additional video).

Aurora Publications
7440 White Ash Place
Parker, Colorado 80134-5464
Telelphone (303) 841-8766

Name: _____

Company: _____

Address: _____

City: _____ State: _____ Zip: _____

PAYMENT: ☒ Check   Ⓒ VISA   Ⓒ MasterCard

Card # _____ Exp. Date: ___/____

Name on Card (if different from above) _____

Order Form

Satisfaction guaranteed or return any books for a full refund.

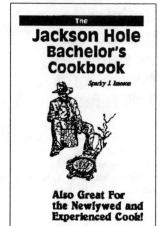

The
Jackson Hole Bachelor's Cookbook

Sparky J. Imeson

Also Great For the Newlywed and Experienced Cook!

Please send _____ copies of:

The Jackson Hole Bachelor's Cookbook

Enclosed is $8.95 plus $1.75 shipping
(75 cents for each additional book).

Aurora Publications
7440 White Ash Place
Parker, Colorado 80134-5464
(303) 841-8766

Name: _____

Company: _____

Address: _____

City:_____ State_____ Zip_____

Payment: ☐ Check ☐ VISA ☐ MasterCard

Card #_____ Exp. Date:_____

Name on Card_____
(If different from above)